ON BEING A WRITER

ann kroeker

&

charity singleton craig

masters in fine living series

ts T. S. Poetry Press • New York

Table of Contents

Appendix 5

Introduction

Is your writing life all it can be? Have you wondered when you'll discover the secrets to find inspiration, improve your skills, get published where you wish, and be part of a real writing community?

Writers can feel both excited and confused about where to start, what to do, how to keep writing. Deep inside, a story itches to be told through personal narrative or fiction, ideas beg to be explored in essays, images ask to be played with, and conflicts yearn to be expressed. We want to do the work—to write—and one day find our words inked on a page or shared at a space online where we know others visit and read. In her book *The Forest for the Trees*, Betsy Lerner quotes John Updike as he recalls his childhood wish to write, to enter "some transfigured mode of being, called a 'writer's life.'"

How do we enter in? How do we experience that transfigured mode? How do we live a "writer's life"?

Because we come at this business from several angles—author, editor, writing coach—people often ask us about that. They want to hear about our writing lives and get a vision for their own. *How did you find your publishers? Should I self-publish? How do I write a query and proposal? What about agents—how do you get one?* And, *I want to be a writer. How do I get started?*

Great questions. People dream of writing and wonder how to launch. Some are drafting manuscripts but don't know how the publishing world works. Others have finished a project and want to take the next step but the process seems confusing. Some writers reach a plateau—they may have published an essay in a journal, or found a publishing home for a book, arrived at some level of online success—and still, they have questions about sustaining themselves over the long haul and creating a writing life that will last.

With this book, we offer a mini-conference to encourage and point the way to a long and productive writing life, by modeling that life and, chapter by chapter, suggesting habits to develop. As authors and editors, we'll be by your side on every page, like your very own writing coaches.

Whether you're developing a corporate, literary, or web-based (blogging and microblogging) body of work, we think you'll benefit from thinking broadly about your writing life and how to organize the rest of your life around your writing goals in a sustainable way. You want the writing life to last your whole life, right? Let's think that through. Together.

Why Another Writing Book?

A sustainable writing life is built from more than the construction of sentences and paragraphs; it emerges from the slow accumulation of days and years lived intentionally through the habits of the writer. This book enumerates, elaborates, and encourages writers regarding key habits. It aims to inspire you toward a writing life that's about more than publishing a book or accumulating by-lines. Though we hope this book will help you find your way toward productivity and publication, we also hope these words help you understand yourself better, learn to set limits, and find rest.

The content of this book was originally developed in a workshop that Ann and Charity led for a group of 12 writers at various stages in their writing lives, all trying to make progress.

An unexpected thing happened while we were leading that workshop. We, too, made progress in our writing lives. Ann transitioned from writing and editing to also coaching others. Charity planned, prepared, and quit her day job and now works as a full-time freelance writer and editor.

We aren't promising you'll make the same moves as a result of buying this book. What we hope is that you'll make the progress you want by reading this book, doing the exercises, and thinking deeply about the writing life you already have.

Who Are We?

Ann Kroeker graduated from Indiana University as an English Major with a creative writing emphasis. She launched her freelance writing career as a young adult and has been working for over two decades as a writer, editor, and most recently as a writing coach. Author of two books and editor for *Tweetspeak Poetry* and *The High Calling*, Ann is a sought-after resource for editorial guidance. She continues to explore new writing opportunities, speak in a range of venues, maintain connections in the publishing world, and work with writers to help them take the next step in their writing careers.

Charity Singleton Craig graduated from Taylor University as a Mass Communications Major with an emphasis in print media. After a brief stint in newspaper journalism, Charity worked in several other industries, all while attempting to live the writing life. She is a freelance writer and editor, serving as a content and copy editor for *The High Calling,* a contributing writer for *Tweetspeak Poetry*, and a staff writer for *The Curator*. She also serves the communication needs of various corporate clients.

How to Use This Book

The book is divided into twelve chapters, each representing habits of the writing life. You might be tempted to think the chapters represent a linear progression toward a successful writing career, and for some people, that may be true. Still, if the writing life were a cake, every slice you'd cut would contain a bit of all twelve layers.

As you read, you'll notice a few components to every chapter. First, the Stories. In the beginning of each chapter, Ann and Charity explore the theme through their own writing lives. We've indicated who is writing within the first or second paragraph in parentheses. When the first narrator is finished, you'll see a divider, then the second narrator will begin. We hope our stories will model the nuances each person brings to the writing life.

After the stories, you'll find an exploration section. Here we suggest opportunities to contemplate, write about, and develop the various habits of the writing life.

Live: Each chapter's exploration begins with *living*—an activity to get you moving and interacting with your writing life. We hope this reinforces the idea that the writing life is wholistic and organic, not compartmentalized, like a job or a hobby.

Respond: A journal prompt gets you writing about what you're thinking and experiencing through the chapter. By responding in a journal first, you can work out your thoughts in a private space that won't be edited or shared.

Write: A writing prompt is offered to help you develop a project to consider sharing on a blog or submitting for publication. If you're reading this book in a group, the prompt might be something you share with other members. For short stories or essays you're writing on your own or planning to submit for publication, aim for a word count of 1,000 words or more. If you're participating in a group and will be reading each other's work, 500-word essays or short stories would be a reasonable goal. Sometimes, we suggest writing a poem. In that case, the word count could be considerably shorter.

Bonus: For writers at every stage of the writing life, we offer another living or writing activity to help you dig deeper into a chapter or topic that really captured your imagination.

Discuss: Finally, in each chapter we provide a few questions to encourage self-reflection or group discussion. These are also useful as additional journaling or writing prompts.

A few ways you might consider engaging with this book:

- Read it with your writing group
- Read a chapter a week, committing to do all of the explorations as you go
- Read straight through and do all the explorations later
- Invite a friend to join you
- Create an online writing group, read the book together, and post writing explorations as a blog link up
- Use it as your personal writing coach, encouraging you to make progress in tangible, practical ways

1

Identify

I am a writer.

If you wish to be a writer, write.

—Epictetus

Stories

Most mornings, I (Ann) pull on shorts and a tank top, lace up my Brooks® trainers, and head out the door. I don't follow a plan to improve my pace or hit particular goals; I'm just trying to stay fit and healthy. Am I a jogger, or can I call myself a runner?

In the past, I've signed up for races and committed to speed work, hills, and tempo runs to work toward a personal best. When I took the activity more seriously, did that make me a runner? Even when training, I was slow—so slow that during a half marathon, I was passed by a much older woman who was power walking. Can a runner call herself a runner if she's passed by a walker?

My husband, who straps on an athletic heart monitor to pace the intensity of his workouts and follows a disciplined training plan, thinks of himself as a runner. Still, people debate definitions. Some would argue that he is a jogger because his pace is too slow, while others would say he's a runner as long as he identifies as one.

What criteria apply here? Is it about speed? Giftedness? Goals? What makes a runner a runner?

I'd like to know the same about writing. What makes a writer a writer? Is it about giftedness? Goals? Is it about output or a byline? If measured by output, does daily blogging count? Are you considered a writer only if you are published, even if you've turned out dozens of unpublished poems and essays? To be an official writer, does someone have to pay you for your work?

I came across a description of "runner" on a discussion board that referred to characteristics of intent and effort. A runner demonstrates intent by entering a race and seeking to finish it strong and fast. To do so, that runner will exert effort by logging many miles in preparation, strengthening his muscles, stretching, eating well, getting appropriate rest. Prioritizing these activities and committing to making them happen separates the recreational or fitness jogger from the serious runner. I read that to my husband, and we agreed that while I'm in it for fitness, he models intent and effort with his running every day. Given that, I'm a jogger and my husband is a runner.

Applying similar criteria to the writing life, however, I model intent and effort every day. I launch projects with intentions that require effort to complete. I plan, research, write, and edit, always seeking to improve. I prioritize these activities and commit to making them happen. Whether or not I earn a byline or paycheck, I continually demonstrate the intent and effort of a writer.

Some people, however—despite their intent and effort—still struggle to identify as a writer. Maybe they believe it takes more. Or maybe they fear friends will think it's frivolous and family will disapprove. Maybe they're missing that moment or event they can point to that says, "That's when I knew I was a writer."

In *Bird by Bird*, Anne Lamott points to that writing-conscious moment in her life. She describes how her second-grade teacher singled out Anne's poem about John Glenn and read it aloud to the class:

> It was a great moment; the other children looked at me as though I had learned to drive. It turned out that the teacher had submitted the poem to a California state schools competition, and it had won some sort of award. It appeared in a mimeographed collection. I understood immediately the thrill of seeing oneself in print. It provides some sort of primal verification: you are in print; therefore you exist.

While I have demonstrated intent and effort for decades, I do find myself pointing to a moment like that, in college.

In my creative writing course, I was churning out poems based on childhood memories, one after another. One afternoon, the teacher dismissed the class but asked me to wait. After the other students grabbed their backpacks and cleared the room, she suggested I submit some of my work to *Labyrinth*, our university's undergraduate literary journal. A literary journal sounded too fancy for me. I wrote poems about window wells, communion, and my grandmother's calico cat. Still, I listened as she told me where to buy a copy. I thanked her, grabbed my backpack, left the room, and headed straight to the Student Union feeling flushed, nerves prickling both arms. I found the current edition of *Labyrinth* sitting on a small table in the bookstore. I felt the glossy cover and flipped through its pages, scanning some poems. I hesitated. *Labyrinth* seemed reserved for smarter, more academic people.

Couldn't hurt to buy it, though. I plopped down my money at the counter and carried the journal back to my room. I found instructions for submission printed on one of the inside pages, and with a wild fear surging all the way to my fingertips, I retyped my favorite poems, printed them off, and tucked them in an envelope. My earthy work in a literary journal? Crazy. And yet, I found the *Labyrinth* office and dropped off the envelope in a metal in-box marked "Submissions."

The journal contacted me and asked to publish four poems. *Four.* A hush of awe, even shock, stunned me silent. Then I turned giddy. The publisher asked for a bio, so I looked at examples from that last edition. The poets talked about why they write. Without over-thinking it, I scribbled out, "I write, because no one listens to me."

Within a few weeks, the next edition of *Labyrinth* published. When they sent me a package of complimentary copies, I pulled one out and ran my fingers over its slick cover. I flipped through and found my poems about window wells, communion, and my grandmother's calico cat.

I felt it inside: *I am a writer.*

If you demonstrate the intent and effort of a writer day after day yet hesitate to refer to yourself as such, take time to reflect on your journey. You might realize you've crossed a threshold, or identified a moment, or experienced an event that affirms you in this role. Whether it was the moment you plopped down money to subscribe to a literary journal, emailed a query to an agent, or received that first acceptance letter, there comes a time when you feel like a writer.

Maybe that moment is now. You bought a book called *On Being a Writer* because you're ready. You've invested in your writing life, showing intent. I'm guessing you've already demonstrated effort. If you haven't felt it or said it, it's time. Say it: "I am a writer."

~

"You're a writer?" my (Charity's) stepson asked me before I married his dad. He was 11 then, and had never met a writer. He was a bit awestruck. Then, the question: "So what do you write?" In that moment, I fell abruptly off the pedestal he'd briefly set me on, knowing that unless I was someone he had heard of or read, like Mary Pope Osborne writing volume after volume of the *Magic Tree House* series, *writer* wouldn't hold the same allure.

I didn't mind. I've been a writer for a long time, and I'm comfortable with having to qualify what I mean.

"Have you written a book?" some people ask—not necessarily because they think all writers write books, but because they would like to know someone who has written a book. I usually tell them "yes." Occasionally, I also confess that the two books I've written have never been published. That's changed with the release of this one.

I honestly don't remember when I started calling myself a writer. I know it was after I had already been a staff writer for a newspaper, after I had written dozens of newsletter articles for various organizations, after I had submitted queries to a dozen or more magazines and been rejected, after I had starting writing a book, after I quit my job to try to write full-time, after I had submitted a successful query to a magazine I loved, and after I was published several times. Needless to say, I could have started calling myself a writer much sooner.

The most difficult part of taking on the identity of writer came during a season when the words dried up and my confidence shriveled.

It started with a rejection, a big rejection for a book I thought was going to be published. In my tailspin, I didn't write anything but a blog post or two for a whole summer. An article I was supposed to be writing at the time, for which I had a lovely outline and a killer thesis, remains largely unwritten to this day.

In the midst of all that non-writing, something else happened. I stopped telling people I was a writer. I began to believe I didn't have what it takes. Not only did I lack the talent needed to be published—the languishing book proposal made that clear—I also seemed to be missing the heart of a long-term writer.

What is required to call oneself a writer? Is it enough simply to put down words? Does a publishing credit or two, or a book in print allow us to claim this title? What of those writers who composed a bestseller and then didn't write again? Could Harper Lee, who wrote the classic *To Kill a Mockingbird* but little else, be called a writer?

Questions fly when we wonder what to call ourselves. After the questions and doubts come, hopefully so do the words. That's what happened when I stopped calling myself a writer. Eventually I started writing again: a blog post every few weeks, then a magazine submission. Other writers I knew encouraged me, link-ing to my blog and asking me to join collaborative projects. About two years later, I found myself in a group of new acquaintances, admiring a piece of artwork one of them created. My comments on the painting caused one man to wonder about my artistic abilities.

"Are you an artist?" he asked, innocently.

"Oh no, no," I said, embarrassed. "I'm not an artist. I just like to paint and draw now and then. But," I added as an afterthought, "I am a writer." He nodded politely. He, of course, asked me what I write. I answered in the usual way: blog posts, online articles, and always a book in progress.

The significance of the moment passed right over him, but to me it was a bellwether.

I lived a writing life long before I ever called myself a writer. But in the last few years, as I have firmly grasped my identity, I have found my life taking the shape of a writer. It's different than I imagined when I was 14, then 22, then 32, dreaming of a life with words.

It's my writing life, and I wouldn't trade it.

Exploration

Live

Says Betsy Lerner:

> To be a writer, to come out of the closet, is to announce that you are different in some way. Until a writer is established and thus somewhat protected by the veneer of success that publication brings, his life and his struggle to emerge

can be fraught with humiliation….Calling attention to yourself, especially within a family dynamic, may involve more scrutiny than a writer can bear. Is there anything worse than being introduced, at a family wedding, for instance, as "our daughter, she's trying to be a writer." Or having some drunken uncle slap you on the back and ask with a loud laugh how the book's coming along?

Fear of this kind of humiliation can keep us from from taking on the writer's identity. Today's *Live* exploration calls you to try on the identity in a low-risk way.

• If this identity as writer feels new...

Tell someone supportive—someone you trust—that you're a writer. Be prepared to explain your new identity.

Then tell someone whose response you're nervous about. Maybe this is your boss, parent, or a friend who is also a writer, and you don't know how to initiate the conversation. If this person is local, meet him for lunch and tell him your hobby has grown and you're doing more with your words than musing in journals. "I want to share this news with you because of how important you've been to me, investing in my creative life." Or share something you've written and explain that you've been a writer secretly for a long time. Whoever it is, you can say, "Thank you for being part of my life and contributing to this writing identity." Stay strong, in case they criticize. Just you wait. Soon enough, these people will start introducing you as their writer-friend.

• If you already identify as a writer...

Think of someone you could affirm as a writer. Contact this person and refer to something he or she has written—an email, blog post, or poem—complimenting the writer's ability and identity.

Respond

Depending on the *Live* assignment you completed, use the appropriate response below to write a journal entry.

Prompt 1: When I told _____ I was a writer . . .

Prompt 2: When I told _____ he/she excelled at _____, he/she . . .

Write

Write about your identity as a writer in personal essay format. Address questions such as: When did you start calling yourself a writer? If you don't yet, what keeps you from it?

Bonus

In your journal, respond to this question: How does rehearsing your story (see: *Write*) help you understand yourself as a writer? Do you feel more like a writer? Or less?

Also, begin writing childhood memories all this week. Start with your earliest memories and capture scenes in descriptive detail that taps all the senses. When you've exhausted the preschool years, move on to the elementary grades.

Discuss

For self-reflection or group discussion.

1. What comes to mind when you think *writer*?

2. When did you first call yourself a writer? If you haven't yet identified as a writer, why not?

3. What other identities have you embodied? Do those identities conflict with the writing life?

4. To what extent do others view you as a writer? How supportive are they of your writing identity? How does outside support—or lack of it—affect your writing identity?

5. Does the kind of writing you produce affect your ability to identify as a writer? Do you feel you need to transition to a more substantial project or different subject matter?

6. Why do you write? What motivates you? How does that influence your identity as a writer?

7. Do you distinguish a difference between an author and a writer? If so, explain the difference and how your identity is affected by those differences.

2

Arrange

I organize my life—
my time, my space, my priorities—so I can write.

The secret of all victory
lies in the organization of the non-obvious.

—Marcus Aurelius

Stories

Crumbling foundations are all that remain of the ancient Puebloan village in Petrified Forest National Park, but just a few steps away, myriad whimsical images cover huge rocks as high as a person can reach. As I (Ann) attach my long lens to get close-ups of these petroglyphs etched into stone, a man standing nearby announces to anyone within earshot, "Someone sure had a lot of time on his hands!" He repeats it, because no one responds. "Someone sure had a lot of time on his hands!"

I know he's trying to be funny, but I ignore him, trying to capture as many digital images of these figures and shapes as possible. Then, as I shift position to focus on a grouping that includes footprints and spirals, I wonder if the man is right: maybe the artist was someone with lots of time on his or her hands, free to make any design that struck a fancy. Or maybe, someone had to *make* time after returning from a hunting or fishing expedition.

We don't know. All we can see is that someone from the village prioritized the making of art. The buildings—necessary for shelter at the time—have crumbled; the art remains.

To make *my* art—writing—I have spent most of my life working around day-to-day family obligations, writing in available slivers of time or slipping away for a while to enjoy an uninterrupted space for creativity. I like to imagine someone from this ancient village doing the same, slipping away after the morning meal or the afternoon washing to put the finishing touches on the outline of a bird or the last swirls of a spiral design. If those artists could pull it off in these dry, barren conditions a thousand years ago, surely I can finish my writing projects in my comfortable, 21st century American abode. Inspired, I resolve to continue arranging my life to accommodate my art.

In the former dining room, I sit at a rolltop desk next to a tall bookshelf. This area dedicated to my work represents and celebrates my priority. This writing life is not an afterthought; it is who I am and what I do. As a result, I occupy a prominent room on our main floor.

Because I work from home, I have to navigate around the family, powering up the computer to write during pockets of time that open up in my day. I remember envying author rituals Barbara Kingsolver describes in *High Tide in Tucson*, like William Gass devoting a couple of hours each morning to photographing his city, and Diane Ackerman arranging flowers, listening to music, and then speed walking for an hour—all preparation for writing. These rituals created space and rhythm.

Kingsolver jokes that her muse "wears a baseball cap, backward. The minute my daughter is on the school bus, he saunters up behind me with a bat slung over his shoulder and says oh so directly, 'Okay, author lady, you've got six hours till that bus rolls back up the drive. You can sit down and write, now, or you can think about looking for a day job.'"

I'm like that, too; I can't wait for inspiration to hit. When I have a few minutes, I have to tap out words. For years, when my kids were young, I felt like Lucille Clifton. When asked "Why are your poems always short?" Kingsolver says that Ms. Clifton replied, "I have six children, and a memory that can hold about twenty lines until the end of the day."

I can't even hold that many lines all day, so I use technology—simple as a pen or high-tech as a voice note—to capture the gist of an idea when continuous writing is not possible. Facing big deadlines, however, I do carve out blocks of time to work, away from the hubbub (or I send the hubbub away). In fact, when working on books, I've been known to schedule a weekend hideout, ensuring uninterrupted time to churn out as many chapter drafts as possible.

Through it all, I try to maintain physical health, because I've learned from personal experience and from research that wise dietary choices, hydration, adequate rest, and especially exercise not only counterbalance the hours I sit in a chair to write, but also ignite creativity. John Medina reports that exercise energizes us:

> From an evolutionary perspective, our brains
> developed while working out, walking as many
> as 12 miles a day. The brain still craves that ex-

perience, especially in sedentary populations like our own. That's why exercise boosts brain power . . . in such populations. Exercisers out-perform couch potatoes in long-term memory, reasoning, attention, and problem-solving tasks.

Information like that inspires me to arrange my life to include exercise like jogging and—try not to laugh, because I swear it loosens my back after long hours in the chair—hula hooping. Physical activity boosts my brain power and keeps me fit to pursue the writing life now and for the years ahead.

Healthy choices like exercise and rest aren't the only things that can increase my creative and cognitive potential. When my schedule is more leisurely, I've experimented with process, space, and time of day for optimal writing output. I drink coffee, I try tea. I read somewhere that chewing helps concentration, so I pop a stick of gum in my mouth. I've tacked up a whiteboard to track to-do lists and later tried sticking Post-it® notes all over my desk. I've used outlines for some projects and then tried freewriting my first draft for others.

Some people insist on writing longhand—I find it effective for poetry but not for nonfiction. Others enjoy the nostalgia and mechanical response of typewriters. In fact, actor—and writer—Tom Hanks claims to be a typewriter man. With apologies to Tom, I prefer the computer. I don't care if my MacBook® keys sound wimpy as I type—on a keyboard, my fingers can keep up with the ideas spilling out of my brain. On a typewriter, they cannot.

William Zinsser observes we all work differently. From his classic book *On Writing Well*:

[T]here isn't any "right" way to do such intensely personal work. There are all kinds of writers and all kinds of methods and any method that helps people to say what they want to say is the right method for them.

Some people write by day, others by night. Some people need silence, others turn on the radio. Some write by hand, some by typewriter or word processor, some by talking into a tape recorder. Some people write their first draft in one long burst and then revise; others can't write the second paragraph until they have fiddled endlessly with the first.

Reading Zinsser makes me feel better about rearranging for my ideal conditions. Regardless of the specifics on any given day, arrangements continually evolve to prioritize writing, which pulls me to the computer again and again to say what I need to say.

~

Part of the process of calling myself (Charity) a writer was actually making time to write. In nearly every book I've read about writing, the author would always claim the only way to get better and to create a body of work was to write every day.

But I was single and worked full-time and had to care for the apartment on my own. Friends and family needed my attention, and I happily gave it to them. I also enjoyed going to movies and reading books and volunteering in the community. In other words, I had a lot of things to do every day besides write.

I wanted to be a writer, though, and I wanted to build a body of work. So over the years, I have made lots of choices that reflect writing as a priority. I have done what I could to make my full-time work correspond with it. Early on, I longed for a job that would provide opportunities to practice my craft. For a year and a half after college, I wrote every day as a newspaper reporter. It didn't take long for me to tire of the news cycle and the veil of objectivity that required me to write the news and only the news, leaving my opinions out of it. I enjoyed working on feature stories, but I formulated too many obituaries and covered too many county commissioner meetings in those 18 months to see a long-term career emerging.

After that, I envisioned a career that would provide something important to write about. I enrolled in graduate school, toying with the idea of becoming a university professor. I worked at a church overseeing children's and women's ministries. I spent two years employed at a small urban college as a residence hall director. These jobs offered many rewards; some of the relationships I built there continue. My writing, however, suffered.

Eventually I learned the full-time work that best complemented my writing didn't involve writing or interacting with a lot of people at all. Whatever part of me I draw on to motivate and inspire me could not be busy eight hours a day and then be expected to produce my own writing in the mornings or evenings as well. I just didn't have that kind of creative energy.

When I took a job working with databases, running queries and creating spreadsheets and macros that aggregated revenues, I realized these exercises in math and logic required a creativity of their own but didn't draw from the same spring as my writing. After a full day of work, I still had something to give.

I've also experimented with my work schedule. My employers have been flexible, allowing me to come in early and leave early so I could write in the afternoons—or come in late and leave late so that I could write in the mornings. When I moved an hour away from the office, I began working part-time from home three days a week, freeing me up for freelance writing and editing. Finally, after a lot of planning and saving, I am self-employed, spending all my work days at home.

Work life aside, there are other ways I have attempted to arrange my life so I can write. I regularly decline commitments to friends, community organizations, family, and others—even commitments I want to make—in favor of more time to write, especially in the face of deadlines.

Sometimes, I wonder whether I lead an indulgent life, neglecting other good work or allowing relationships to suffer for my art. It's possible, but on the flipside there are times when the writing must wait because I choose to spend the evening with my husband, or I must go visit my uncle in the hospital, or I have to do the grocery shopping so we can eat breakfast the next day.

How to find balance?

In his essay "The Specialization of Poetry," Wendell Berry talks about this pull we feel between our daily lives and the work we do, especially as artists.

> The conflicts of life and work, like those of rest and work, would ideally be resolved in balance: enough of each. In practice, however, they probably can be resolved (if that is the word) only in tension, in a principled unwillingness to let go of either, or to sacrifice either to the

other. But it is a necessary tension, the grief in
it both inescapable and necessary. . . . The real
values of art and life are perhaps best defined
and felt in the tension between them.

As a full-time writer, I wrestled this weekend with the tension of
giving myself fully to the work or fully to my life. Yesterday, instead
of working on this manuscript, I took the day off to enjoy dinner and bowling with my husband and sons. Today, however,
I am working, and they are all huddled around the television for
a movie without me. Yesterday, I felt the tug of work, today, the
tug of family. As the years come and go, I continue to make
adjustments to schedules, adding or subtracting commitments,
letting the writing lead me in how much time I should spend.
But always, always, I am attempting to arrange my life in such a
way that this writing life is more than just a dream.

"How we spend our days is, of course, how we spend our
lives," Annie Dillard says in *The Writing Life*. "What we do with
this hour, and that one, is what we are doing. A schedule defends
from chaos and whim. It is a net for catching days. It is a scaf-
folding on which a worker can stand and labor with both hands
at sections of time."

I arrange my life so I can write.

Exploration

Live

Do you have a writing space? Do you have a set time, set hours?
Does your space, time and hours match your inner rhythm and
personality? Your answers to these questions reflect the degree to

which you have prioritized your writing life and honored how you work best.

Evaluate your writing space. What's working, what's not? As much as possible, remove the things that steal your energy, distract, or frustrate you (an outdated photograph, a pile of unsorted papers, the mass of cords jumbled at your feet, the stack of unpaid bills staring you in the face). Then, rearrange what remains to improve productivity and inspiration. Finally, decide if you need to add something—anything from a bookshelf to an ergonomically designed desk chair (you will, after all, spend hours in it); from a piece of art or a plant to a new printer—and incorporate it into your space. Write in your new space this week and make adjustments as needed.

Now consider your schedule. What other commitments keep you from writing? What simple adjustments could free up at least 30 minutes to write each day? Maybe you could delegate a household chore to someone else, or skip a TV show? Could you reduce social media time or cancel one outing? Maybe you could set your alarm clock to wake up 30 minutes early or stay up a little later, adding 15-30 minutes to the phase when your body rhythm is peaking?

How flexible is your lifestyle? What time of day best complements your personality and energy levels? Try to accommodate activities so that writing occurs at a peak time for maximum productivity.

Schedule "Writing" on your calendar. Commit to it. Tell others about it. When the schedule says to write, write. Stick with your new habit for one month and see how it goes. Some days will go better than others. When you wake up later than intended or spend your time clicking through *Buzzfeed* slideshows, try again the next day, and the next, until writing in that 30-minute window becomes a habit. If you find after several weeks it really isn't working, experiment to find a time that will work better for you. This is your writing life; you'll need to find what fits you.

Respond

As you consider how to rearrange your space (see *Live*), freewrite for ten minutes responding to this prompt: "My perfect writing day would . . ." Include as much rich sensory detail and specificity as possible. Think more broadly than your physical space to include how you would arrange your daytime hours, your activities, your weekends.

After you rearrange, live with, and work in the new surroundings for a day or two, write about it in your journal using the prompt: "My new writing space . . ."

Write

Write a short piece about jealousy regarding other writers—how you envy their eclectic, organized writing spaces that look far more inspiring than yours, perhaps, or maybe their part-time job that gives them full afternoons to devote to writing. If a short essay doesn't express the emotions or intensity of what you need to say, try writing a poem.

Jealousy is a powerful emotion to stir up in any stage of the writing life; yet, expressing these thoughts can help identify your deepest desires about the writing life and how you wish you were living it. Use the jealousy as a teacher and a source of beginning to change, rather than letting it trap you in guilty feelings you may have been taught to associate with the experience of jealousy.

Bonus

What long-term commitment can you make to cement this writing-life arrangement? Have you been considering writing full-time? Have you thought of a plan to move forward? Some may need to hire a babysitter once a week; others may need to sell their house and move into an apartment to simplify life. Decide what makes sense for you and write those ideas down. Create a plan that moves you closer to that vision. Whether you pursue that plan all at once or in stages, ensure you make progress this week.

Discuss

For self-reflection or group discussion.

1. To what extent have you arranged your space and time to honor your writing?

2. How does your schedule support or challenge your writing life?

3. What are your challenges and successes in the area of time management? How about project and task management?

4. What tangible arrangements can you (and your family or roommates, if applicable) make to allow you to pursue the writing life more easily and productively?

5. Do you think it's necessary to write every day? Why or why not?

6. If you do write daily, what do you feel it accomplishes in your writing life: improvement of the craft? Adding to your body of work? Professional discipline?

3

Surround

*I surround myself with people,
activities, and books that will
influence my writing.*

If you have other things in your life—
family, friends, good productive day work—
these can interact with your writing
and the sum will be all the richer.

—David Brin

Stories

It was a Wednesday evening and my new husband and I (Charity) were home by ourselves. My slow adaptation to married life and motherhood now that I was a stepmom to 10-, 12-, and 14-year-old boys frustrated me. I was 42, and married for the first time.

"Would you be interested, or at least willing, to go to an exhibit at the art museum Saturday?" I asked my husband. Part of my difficulty in adjusting to marriage was the realization that I had set aside everything I liked to do to fit into my new role. I was living someone else's life, one that wasn't satisfying to me personally, and it was choking out my writing life. All I was writing about was motherhood and marriage during those first few months. Where had the rest of my life gone?

"Sure," he said, willing, even eager. He mentioned, as well, an art fair in the same city going on that Saturday. Almost a year earlier, he had taken me to an art exhibit on our second date. He remembers, maybe better than I do, who I was—and still am.

On Saturday, we drove to the art museum and not only took in the Ai Weiwei exhibit but also became members of the museum, a commitment from both of us that we would surround ourselves with what inspires me to write. It worked. Within a couple of weeks, I wrote on my blog about that conversation we had in the kitchen, submitted a review of the exhibit to *Tweetspeak Poetry,* and planned two more articles based on the museum membership.

Writing requires a flow both inward and outward of ideas, thoughts, and stories. Each time I write an essay or an article, I gather together everything I know, think, and experience about the topic, sorting and synthesizing, squeezing together bits of inspiration and searching for just the right combination of words. Sometimes, when I'm done writing a piece, I discover a quote or a story that didn't quite fit. Perhaps it is enough material for one more piece.

Eventually, I'll have to write about something else, and if I'm not surrounding myself with people and books and experiences that inspire and connect with me, I may be left wondering what to write about. If I'm surrounding myself with people, books, and experiences that drain me or leave me lifeless, I will have only that to write about. Even worse, if the bits and pieces of my daily life leave me uninspired, I will have nothing left to write.

In *The Writing Life*, Annie Dillard talks about the importance of surrounding ourselves with whatever inspires us. The writer, she says, "is careful of what he reads, for that is what he will write. He is careful of what he learns, because that is what he will know." If we write about and become what we surround ourselves with, it would make sense to actively choose in particular directions.

In her essay "The Writing Life," author Geraldine Brooks talks about the experience of writing her first novel. She had intended to write about her homeland of Australia, but instead she found the stories of England she had read and dreamed about her whole life were waiting for her pen.

> It was to have been set in Tasmania, amid the wild temperate rain forests of Australia's southernmost state. Instead, I found myself writing about Derbyshire. The fictional voices in my head were English voices, and they kept shouting the Australians down. There was a story that had intrigued me for years, of a village that voluntarily quarantined itself to stop the spread of bubonic plague. It was this tale, rather than the Australian one, that most wanted to be told.

Brooks, like Dillard, knows that what she surrounds herself with is what she writes. That's why she says if she is ever going to write about Australia, even though it's her homeland, she will need to study. "I will have to learn it, like a foreigner, like a migrant, leaf by leaf, from seed to blossom to bough."

In *The New York Times Opinionator* blog post "Should We Write What We Know?" Ben Yagoda believes this is the beautiful freedom of the "write what you know" motto. It's true, he says, that "writers who are intimately familiar with their subject produce more knowing, more confident and, as a result, stronger results. . . . but that command is not perfect, implying, as it does, that one's written output should be limited to one's passions."

"Fortunately, this conundrum has an escape clause," Yagoda continues. "You can actually acquire knowledge. In journalism this is called 'reporting,' and in nonfiction, 'research.' I don't write fiction, but I'd think that a rigorous combination of observation, reflection and directed imagination would have a similar result."

I have been married about two years now. I watch far more sports and reality television than I ever did, but I also have begun reading more again and going to art exhibits and listening to National Public Radio in the mornings when I work. I've filled my office with things that inspire me: newspaper articles, like the one I clipped about a local sports hero; a Matisse print from the art museum gift shop; and books about birds, trees, and poetry that help me make sense of the world. I have conversations with friends about the economy and literature. Then when I go running—I'm doing that more now, too—I let my brain have time to sort it all out.

These are the things I want to write about, so I surround myself with them.

~

My (Ann's) parents surrounded me with books. Almost every room in the house was lined with shelves weighed down with classics and review copies of books they received at *The Indianapolis Star*, where they both worked as editors. They didn't let me read the hardbound Heritage Editions of the classics that each slid into their own matching cardboard sleeves—Dad, especially, was afraid I'd crack the spine or spill Kool-Aid® on the pages. He was probably right to be concerned. I was allowed to read all the rest, and they bought me children's books I devoured, like Dr. Seuss and the Marguerite Henry horse books. Mom let me read her entire collection of Trixie Belden, The Bobbsey Twins, and her personal copy of *Anne of Green Gables*. Books became friends.

But I wanted to read even more widely, following whims and figuring things out. I craved books on every topic that interested me. With permission to open them wide and read, while slurping lemonade, I needed a library.

Mom regularly drove me to town and deposited me in that dreamy place where I could search the stacks for anything that intrigued. The library gave me the freedom to check out books on any topic, and no one seemed to mind if I opened the spine a little too wide. I began to learn, laugh, and connect with everyone from Nancy Drew and the Hardy Boys to *Little Women*'s Jo. From piles of nonfiction books I learned about writing, painting, calligraphy, photography, fitness, terrariums, the care and keeping of crickets, and how to bake homemade bread. Books became more than friends. They became mentors.

When we were first married, my husband set up shelves and I filled them with books collected from Goodwill and Friends of the Library sales. I amassed memoirs, novels, and classics, especially titles I remembered from the Heritage Editions, so I could fill in those gaps and read what I'd missed along the way. When we had kids, I picked up nonfiction titles on parenting and education, creativity, fitness, and gardening, trying to parent well while keeping my "self" alive in the early days of motherhood.

As I began to build a more intentional writing life, I filled the library of my mind with quality prose and poetry. Often I immersed myself in an author's rhythm, and my own work would include hints of her tone and cadence. Even her content might influence mine. Annie Dillard's *Pilgrim at Tinker Creek* offered a literary-rich contemplative model; Madeleine L'Engle's nonfiction demonstrated an intelligent, creative, curious approach to life; Anne Lamott freed me to write honestly; Lauren Winner and Haven Kimmel introduced me to the power of memoir.

Stephen King says, "Reading is the creative center of a writer's life." I believe it. I carry these words, these stories, these ideas and styles in me, and they contribute to an ongoing, internal conversation that inspires and influences my writing life.

Don't get me wrong. I enjoy many rich friendships with real-life people who engage me creatively. But a writer needs to surround herself with input and ideas that feed and energize her work, and while friends can often supply that, they shouldn't be expected to fill that role entirely.

This week I pulled off the shelf *Essays of E. B. White*. His writing delights, with stories of pigs, a chimney fire, and Christmas in Florida. When our family was reorganizing the children's bedrooms over the weekend, I found myself reading aloud to my husband White's essay on decluttering his home and how hard he found it to rid himself of trophies and a chip of wood gnawed by a beaver. "This!" I exclaimed. "This is exactly what it's like!"

And this, I thought, *is how I'd like to write.*

I'll finish *Essays of E.B. White* soon, but I want to re-read it to figure out what made each essay work so well. While clearing shelves in the basement, I turned up some art books I plan to leaf through with my son. Perhaps I'll write about that on my blog. Later today I'll ride my bike down the shaded rails-to-trails path that leads over a bridge and then under an overpass, and if I turn left at the ice cream shop, and pass the tea store and then the bank, I'll end up at the library, where, somewhere on the shelves, I expect to collect more books, more ideas, more mentors. I can never have enough.

Exploration

Live

If you write about what you surround yourself with, you can evaluate your life and writing in two ways. First, you could consider what you are writing about and how that connects with the world you inhabit. Second, you could look at the books, people, and places in your life, and how those things are influencing your writing. Are you writing about the things you want to write about?

Evaluate your world: what one thing can you change this week—the things you read, the places you go, the hobbies you enjoy, the conversations you engage in, etc.—that will connect with what you currently are writing or hope to write about? Make that change. For instance, if you are a nurse who spends your days or nights in the hospital but what you really want to write about is antique furniture, are you spending time in antique stores, do you visit auctions or museums, do you subscribe to *Treasures Magazine*? If not, start by making one change.

Respond
Spend ten minutes journaling about the change you made or are planning to make in your life and how you expect it to affect your writing.

Write
According to Annie Dillard, Ernest Hemingway modeled his work after the novels of Knut Hamsun and Ivan Turgenev. Ralph Ellison looked to Hemingway and Gertrude Stein. Henry David Thoreau was inspired by Homer. Eudora Welty loved Anton Chekhov. William Faulkner owed his literary acumen to Sherwood Anderson and James Joyce. Who are your writing heroes?

Write a short essay about a writer whose work you admire or a fictional character whose writing life inspires you. Include aspects of your hero's life, writing style, form, and voice that you admire and how you would like to incorporate them into your work.

Or, if you prefer, write a short story or poem based on the work of your writing heroes, mimicking style or genre, or using your hero as the main character. Remember, if you aren't currently an expert on this writer's life, you can always research to find the nugget that will inspire your writing.

Bonus
Julia Cameron's "Artist Dates" provide a creative way to interact more directly with the people, places, and events you surround yourself with. Plan an Artist Date this week and write about it. If your writing life has become too serious lately, consider choos-

ing a destination that will allow you to have some fun and inject energy into your writing life. *Tweetspeak* has several wonderful resources to get you started, along with samples of the wide range of refreshing outings that could feed your creative spirit. See Appendix 3 for more details.

Discuss

For self-reflection or group discussion.

1. If you set out to write a novel about a culture you are or would like to be steeped in, where would your book be set? What are some of the things you surround yourself with that naturally make their way into your writing without even trying?

2. People are an important part of what surrounds us, but sometimes including other people's stories in our writing can be complicated. How do you deal with mentioning, naming, or describing other people's actions, circumstances, or conversations in your writing? Do you ask permission or seek their interest before you write about them?

3. What are your biggest concerns with writing about other people? Is family harder or easier for you than friends or acquaintances? How will you resolve these concerns?

4. What limitations have you encountered that keep you from surrounding yourself the way you would like? Financial? Geographic? What realistic steps can you take to make the changes you would like?

4

Notice

I attend to and record what's going on around me.

Try to be one of the people
on whom nothing is lost.

—Henry James

Stories

Years ago, I (Ann) read *The Seven Storey Mountain* by Thomas Merton and wondered how on earth he could remember the details of the green verandah and rocking chairs, the banana trees and oleanders, of an island where he lived as a child. I have also marveled at Haven Kimmel's powers of recall in *A Girl Named Zippy*. How did she remember that the man in her neighborhood, Mr. Kizer, wore blue work pants, a white T-shirt, a brown cardigan, and sock feet on the day she dropped by his house with her sister? More recently, Jeannette Walls' powers of recall that formed *The Glass Castle* seem impossible. Among the hundreds of other details she remembers, we learn the full name of a teacher her mom rode to work with (Lucy Jo Rose), where the woman attended college (Bluefield State College), the make and model of the car she drove (a Dodge® Dart), the brand of cigarettes she smoked (Kools), and the music she played to school and back (Barbara Mandrell).

I can barely remember the color of the bathroom walls in my current house, let alone my childhood couch or my high school friend's bedspread. I can walk across the house and remind myself that in a momentary lapse of judgment, I painted our half bath one shade softer than Pepto-Bismol® pink. My mom probably remembers the color of my childhood couch, but I am left to imagine it was plaid or maybe some kind of toile. I can't remember my friend's bedspread, but I'm thinking maybe it was a solid color. I spent a good percentage of my high school years in that room listening to music and discussing the meaning of life, so you'd think I could recreate every detail. I was half-asleep, I guess, or living in the moment without realizing I might like to retain it. In any case, I failed to lock it in.

This tendency to skim through life's details continued into my college and young adult years—even into marriage and parenting. When my son called a pancake a "pampake," I laughed, mussed his hair, and then lifted him out of the booster chair to change his diaper so I could run an errand. I remembered it because I retold the story to a friend later that same day. Plus, he said "pampake" for a long time before he straightened it out. But I wonder how many of those sweet moments have been lost to me because I did not draw them deep into memory.

Though my kids are older now—two have entered college, even—for many years I was consumed by the chaos of four kids' pacifiers and sippy cups, water wings and tricycles. Entire days whizzed past as I wrangled preschoolers, toddlers, and babies. When one of them told a knock-knock joke that made us all laugh, I chuckled, cleared the plates, and then forgot it. I barely noticed material that could have filled a dozen books. I've lost entire years of specific details that would make my writing come alive.

To live more fully during those years when my kids were young, I determined to slow down and practice *noticing*. Somewhere along the line, I started to turn toward my children and look them in the eye, holding their gaze an extra beat or two. I reached out to touch the bark of a sycamore and dip my feet in the cool creek near my house. I literally stopped to smell roses and summersweet, hydrangea and honeysuckle. I began to pay attention to life instead of letting it slip through my fingers. This downshift to a slower gear set our family apart and made me more attentive. Friends and family noticed the change. Neighbors and people at church mentioned it. Our pace grew slow enough that I decided to write about it, chronicling parts of our story in a book called *Not So Fast*.

These days, attention and curiosity work together in my writing life as I notice and wonder. Sometimes, too, I recall. Recalling allows me to draw from my reservoir of memories, those moments when I've noticed and retained something in the past—something worth revisiting (and possibly writing about).

Dorothea Brande suggests a simple way to step out of the oblivion and engage memory:

> [S]et yourself a short period each day when you
> will, by taking thought, recapture a childlike
> "innocence of eye." For half an hour each day
> transport yourself back to the state of wide-
> eyed interest that was yours at the age of five.
> Even though you feel a little self-conscious

> about doing something so deliberately that was
> once as unnoticed as breathing, you will still
> find that you are able to gather stores of new
> material in a short time.

This state of receptivity prepares me to notice the world, but I need to do more than recapture my innocence of eye—I must also pick up a pen and record what I notice.

Some years I've kept a physical journal and filled its pages with sketches, quotations, and descriptions of outings. Or I opened a Word® document at end of the day and added stand-out images and interactions. I've experimented with OneNote®, Evernote® workspace, voice memos, and voice-to-text in Google Drive®. Different situations called for one approach over another. Whatever method I use, this practice helps me think like a writer, explore like a writer, and set it all down like a writer.

On days I don't know what to write about, I search Google Drive. I find a note about chipping paint off my brand-new mirror and craft a blog post about imperfection. I reread a newspaper opinion piece I scanned into OneNote and reference it for an article. I flip through my handwritten journal to review a campground conversation and work it into a poem. I listen to a voice memo to see if it could find its way into a book.

If I remember the past in greater detail and stay receptive to the present, I'm never without material. The things I notice become part of my story; my work becomes more memorable, more textured, more real.

I become one of those people on whom nothing is lost.

~

My husband and I (Charity) were on our way out of town for the weekend, and in the first few minutes of the trip, we passed the county landfill, a giant mountain of garbage that makes the disposable culture of our county and surrounding ones possible.

"Looks like grass is growing on the dump," my husband commented. I looked. Sure enough, this fenced-off pile of garbage was producing patches of green. I tucked the image away in memory, but before we got too far down the road, I pulled a 3x5 notecard from my purse and started writing.

"What are you doing?" he asked.

"Just making a note about the grass growing on the dump," I said. "I might want to write about it."

The dump was more than just *garbage* in my life. The first time I drove to the house we lived in a while once married was when I was still dating him. "You'll turn left at the dump," he'd told me. *How will I recognize it?* I had wondered, not realizing the gargantuan pile was impossible to miss. I smelled it before I saw it, and then encountering its size, knew unmistakably this was the spot. I steered left past the dump, toward my future.

The dump was created in 1996, and according to our city's website, it will be full in less than five years. The Frankfort Environmental Development Company is developing 192 acres across the street from the current dump to accommodate the trash of our future. In 20 years, it, too, will be full.

I didn't know as I was turning left that day how much my life would change. I didn't realize as I drove past the dump that bits of my life would amass there over the next 20 years. I didn't know grass could grow on top of a trash heap of my own making.

I jotted this down, travelling north at 70 miles per hour. With pen and note card still in hand, I recorded another reminder of a thought that had occurred to me while reading an online article. "Wendell Berry was a young man living an alternative lifestyle." That's all I wrote, but it was just enough to remind me of the picture I saw of a young Berry in an article by his daughter in *Edible Louisville*. The article is a touching tribute to the life her father has led since he left academic life to farm in Eastern Kentucky. The problem was the decision was quite public and at times very difficult for a teenage Mary Berry.

> Unfortunately for me, my father didn't understand at all that he should, at the very least, not write about these things and should never mention the composting privy to a journalist. I was in a difficult predicament. I never really thought that my father was wrong about anything. In fact, the reasons for the things we did at home were talked about all of the time, and I understood and even honored those reasons. But, to have details about your composting privy reported in the *Louisville Courier-Journal* was just too much to be borne.

As a Wendell Berry fan, I've read most of what he's written. I even sat at arm's length behind him and shook his wife's hand before and after a lecture he gave at Indiana University. For some reason, I had pictured him always as an old man, reflecting back on a better time. I couldn't shake the image of a handsome, young Wendell Berry I saw in that article.

The card with the note about the grass on the garbage pile and the young Wendell Berry eventually found its way into a drawer next to a sticky note with the word "delight" and a mail flier from a local dentist on which I have notes about pulling weeds and not baking bread.

"Push it. Examine all things intensely and relentlessly," says Annie Dillard in *The Writing Life*. So I don't stop when I notice the heat of a sunny day. I also take note of the warmth rising from damp grass and fields of bright green corn stalks. If I recognize a sweet smell in the air as I ride my bicycle, I look around and find purple clover growing next to Queen Anne's lace and tiny bachelor buttons. Then I write it all down.

Some days, that's the most "writing" I do—jot a note on a circular ad from the mailbox. Later, I sit down and find I have something to work with.

Exploration

Live

Some of us need to train ourselves to see, to be attentive, to listen and sense hints of deeper meaning.

Once we begin to notice the things that stand out for whatever reason (sometimes we don't know why), we need to capture and record what we notice.

Pick your preferred note-taking method—make it something you can always keep with you—and take note of at least three things today. Listen to a voice or a new sound; reach out to touch something you might have passed without taking in that tactile sensation; look more closely, even using binoculars or a magnifying glass for a fresh perspective. Read something you might have simply bookmarked or ignored. Pay attention to many sources: stories that catch your eye in the newspaper, conversations you overhear in the mall restroom, an insect fluttering in the path ahead, the sound of a cuckoo clock chirping the hour.

Of those things you noticed, record at least three. You can use a few words to jog your memory later, or you can write in more detail, to preserve the nuance.

Do the same thing tomorrow and the next day—notice and capture. All this week, capture at least three things per day. Toward the end of the week, spread out your collection of notes, paste them into a document, transcribe them from audio, or handwrite them into a notebook, and decide which ones grab you.

Respond
In your journal, freewrite about one of the things you captured. Ten minutes without stopping. Go.

Write
Use some of your notes to write an essay or a poem, drawing from senses and thoughts that hit you when you made the notes.

Or, visit a favorite place and record responses from all five senses, then describe your favorite place in an observation piece. Assume your reader knows nothing about this location.

Some ideas to add depth:

· Choose a location where other people are part of the environment
· Include details not only about the place itself, but also about the people, the actions, and events
· Use your observations to convey your impression of the spirit or mood of the scene

- Remember you are writing to people who probably have not been to your favorite spot. Write as if to take them there, expressing your unique perspective without falling back on standard descriptions
- Choose details carefully so you can make your point clearly in the space allowed

Bonus

Think of some people in your life for whom you could write a gift of words or story. What might your words be? Decide what story (or stories) you might present as a narrative essay, poem, or series of letters and who will receive it. Start working on it— what might begin as a series of poems or letters could grow into a blog or a book.

Discuss

For self-reflection or group discussion.

1. On a scale of one to ten, how naturally attentive are you? How much do you notice and how much slips by? (*One* means you'd remain lost in a daydream as a herd of elephants rumbled past; *ten* means you see and find meaning in every dust bunny and telephone pole.) Explain.

2. On a scale of one to ten, how easily do you recall details without recording them in some way? Explain.

3. What is your preferred method of recording and storing things you notice?

4. What kind of details are the easiest for you to remember? Colors? Sounds? Smells? How can you improve your awareness of your other senses?

5. What do you think is the problem with including too few details in your writing? Is it possible to include too many details? From your experience as a reader, what authors strike a good balance in their inclusion of sensory details?

5

Write

I sit down and put words to paper.

A writer who waits for ideal conditions
under which to work
will die without putting a word to paper.

—E. B. White

Stories

I (Charity) don't know how else to break it to you: writing is hard. Maybe you already knew that.

Many books have been written on the process and particulars of writing. In *Bird by Bird*, Anne Lamott offers several amusing and insightful prescriptions for getting the words down on paper, like "shitty first drafts" and "one-inch frames." Julia Cameron is known for her "morning pages" in *The Artist's Way*. Stephen King has his "tool box" of trade tricks in *On Writing*. Then, there's Dorothea Brande, who talks about writing on a schedule and a "second wind."

Annie Dillard tells us we need to start with *vision*. But, one reader asked her, *who will teach me to write*? I don't think this reader was looking for a grammar lesson or a how-to on narrative arc or dialog. She wanted to know how to sit down and write, to move herself from the desire to the action. Dillard's response? "The page, the page, that eternal blankness, the blankness of eternity which you cover slowly . . . that page will teach you to write."

Even as I sat down to complete this chapter, the page stared blankly at me. I did everything but the writing I should have been doing. I checked email; I looked over my calendar; I read through some articles at *Tweetspeak*; I did a Google search on a couple of topics; and then, I landed at Facebook, where the chances were good I would linger far beyond my allotted writing time.

As I was reading the status updates, I saw this quote attributed to W. H. Auden scrolling through my feed: "You owe it to all of us to get on with what you're good at." I read it twice through, feeling like Auden himself had just reached through time and grabbed me by the shirt. *Yes, you! Get on with it.*

I quickly logged off and got to work.

Many of us will eventually find what we need to make our writing better. We will come to understand our first drafts aren't perfect and a good editor cuts and polishes. We'll read books and attend workshops and maybe even enroll in a Masters of Fine Art (MFA) program.

Regardless of how well we can write, we'll never become master writers in our own right, unless we sit ourselves down every day—or most days—and just get on with it.

Sitting in my office or perched in front of my laptop at a nearby coffee shop, I feel alone in my struggle to get started. Of course, this isn't true, but why is it so hard to begin? As it turns out, we are compelled to *start* for precisely the same reasons we find the writing hard.

First, we have something to say that can come only from us. Though we often find ourselves, our lives, in the pages of others, what's missing? Where is the story, the perspective, the hope that only I can express? I can look and look for it, but I'll never find it until I sit down and write. Dillard describes this as giving voice to our own astonishment; she reminds us of Anne Truitt's call to work along our "most intimate sensitivity," and of Thoreau's imperative to "know your own bone: gnaw at it, bury it, unearth it, and gnaw at it still."

Finding that thing only I can write about is life-giving; it's not called my "most intimate sensitivity" for nothing. Living in this place of friction can create sparks, but it also causes chafing. When I write about my cancer journey, long-term singleness, or the adjustment to becoming a wife and mother so late in life, my words seem to come alive for readers. They comment about my honesty and unique perspective. But the emotional work required to move these struggles from my heart to the page is tiring and occasionally frightening. Sometimes, I'm not sure it's worth it.

The second reason we resist sitting down to work is we want our writing to be perfect.

Perfection can draw us *to* the work, make us want to write well, give us a goal and a dream. I'm reminded of Madeleine L'Engle's encounter as a girl with the master artists on display at the Metropolitan Museum. Rather than intimidate, they inspired. "A great painting, or symphony, or play, doesn't diminish us, but enlarges us," she says, "and we, too, want to make our own cry of affirmation to the power of creation behind the universe." I have felt that way when reading L'Engle's words. As a young woman encountering her *Pickwick Journals*, I remember thinking:

"I want to write like this." Then, I just started doing it. Not perfectly. Not exactly like her, but inspired by her.

Perfectionism is another problem entirely. It keeps us from the work, convinces us we'll never be good enough, squashes our ambitions. Often, it stops us from putting the first word on a page. For me, perfectionism comes and goes. While I can easily write a blog post on a familiar topic or draft an article for a magazine I've worked with before, new audiences and new topics paralyze me. I spend days—sometimes weeks—outlining, brainstorming, crowdsourcing, and daydreaming. When I force myself to start, even freewriting feels impossible. I'm convinced I can't move into this new space, that what I've got to say isn't brilliant enough. I wonder how I persuaded the editor or publisher I could write. Even now I have a project due in ten days. I know the editor personally; she's confident I can write what she assigned. I have a hard time believing it, though. I have yet to move out of my note-taking phase.

"The bottom line is that if you want to write, you get to," Lamott says. "But you probably won't be able to get very far if you don't start trying to get over your perfectionism." Later today, I'll have to make myself sit down at my laptop. I'll set a timer. I'll begin typing a few tangled paragraphs and hate myself for it. But then I'll remind myself about the article I wrote just last week, the one I struggled with and nearly abandoned. I'll remember it wasn't perfect and the editor had to suggest major restructuring. In the end, though, I'll recall how it turned out well. Then, I'll quit chiding myself and just do the work.

Writing is hard; that's nothing new. But perhaps "you owe it to all of us to get on with what you're good at." It is fine to start with the mere bones.

~

Stephen King insists every writer needs a room with a door. I (Ann) am situated in a room with a desk, a bookshelf, a computer, and a window I can open to let in a breeze, but I don't have a door. In fact, this former dining room boasts two doorways, but neither has a door, so the kids and their friends and the dogs move through this space on their way from the front room to the kitchen. Often someone turns up her music without realizing I'm trying to concentrate. Or my college-aged kids come home and jam to *Guitar Hero*® in the next room. My space is great, but I sure would love some doors.

If I wait for ideal conditions—for all four of my kids to move away to college, or for my husband to install French doors—I'll get nothing done. So I settle into my swivel chair, pop in earbuds to tune out the commotion, and start typing. Or I sescape to another location, even though my desk area is a perfect set-up with my books and printer on hand. The writing must get done, whether or not I have an assignment or deadline. It must get done because I have something to say that nudges until it finds its way onto the page. It must get done because I want to improve and the only way is to keep experimenting, keep taking risks, doing the work, putting down one word after another.

I write when I'm inspired and churn out words like a machine. I write when I'm tired and have to step away from the computer several times to reorient myself. I write when the dog is barking and the wind is whining.

Some things can't be ignored. A thunderstorm blows in, and I run through the house shutting windows; the dog needs to go out when the kids can't help; I have to drive someone to soccer, or the neighbor needs to borrow the mower. When interruptions peck at me like our parakeet tapping the metal bars of his cage (yes, we have a parakeet . . . want one?), the writing stops.

I'm amused by Stephen King's description of a novel in which writers' colony participants stay in cabins in a wooded setting. At noon, someone quietly sets a box lunch on the front stoop, to avoid disrupting the writer's work. In the evenings, men and women gather in front of a fire at the lodge to toast marshmallows, pop popcorn, drink wine, and read their work aloud. This seems "like an absolutely enchanted writing environment." King expands:

> I especially liked the part about having your lunch left at the front door, deposited there as quietly as the tooth fairy deposits a quarter under a kid's pillow. I imagine it appealed because it's so far from my own experience, where the creative flow is apt to be stopped at any moment by a message from my wife that the toilet is plugged up and would I try to fix it, or a call from the office telling me that I'm in imminent danger of blowing yet another dental appointment. At times like that I'm sure all writers feel pretty much the same, no matter what their skill and success level: *God, if only I were in the right writing environment, with the right understanding people, I just KNOW I could be penning my masterpiece.*

In truth, I've found that any day's routine interruptions and distractions don't much hurt

> a work in progress and may actually help it in
> some ways. It is, after all, the dab of grit that
> seeps into an oyster's shell that makes the pearl,
> not pearl-making seminars with other oysters.

I've dreamed of escaping to something like a writer's colony when my days have unfolded like King's, with clogged toilets and forgotten appointments. How reassuring to hear that an author as productive as King has found interruptions don't hurt much and might, in fact, help. I like to believe that days when I maneuver my writing around the mélange of life, my projects turn sharper, cleaner, more effective—even pearl-like, for all the grit seeping in.

Neighbors and friends sometimes ask me to let their dogs out for a midday run or take a leisurely lunch date. Maybe they assume my work-from-home lifestyle means I'm watching HGTV all afternoon. At any rate, I evaluate those requests on a case-by-case basis; I like to help people and nurture friendships, but I also value my goals and associated deadlines enough to say no.

Many professionals keep dedicated work hours or set a word count to achieve their goals and deadlines. For most of my writing life, I wasn't able to pull that off because family obligations evolved from year to year, even day to day, and I couldn't count on set hours. Plus, my personality resists structure. In fact, my spontaneous personality may contribute to the neighbors' and friends' requests.

Recently, though, as I've gained more daytime writing hours, I've established routines for repetitive domestic tasks like laundry and dishes, and I've added a kind of rhythm to my writing and editing. I use a task management system that correlates with a calendar to keep me on track with deadlines. I set a timer to compel me to complete a given task. All of these tools help me commit to the work, persevere when distracted, and simply sit down to write.

When I say "write," I mean the whole process of writing, from initial brainstorming to final edits. Regardless of a writer's workflow, every project moves through a process. First, there's prewriting as I generate ideas by drawing mind maps, making lists, and freewriting. Then I compose a first draft, and refine it, self-editing in practical ways—starting with the high-level view to see if the idea carries through my piece and it's organized in a way that works, later switching to copyediting notes. In successive drafts, I tune my eyes (or the "find" feature in Word) to search for pet words and sentence constructions I tend to overuse and strike them down, searching for some new-to-me expression.

Eventually, I'm close. I often print out the final draft to pick through, the way my childhood neighbor used to pick-pick-pick through beans to hunt for bits of rock or tiny chunks of dirt. This editorial approach can be maddening for anyone who's worked with me. I keep coming back to the words with another tweak. And another. *Hold on*, I think, *I can remove another "that," "but," "just," or "so."*

From conception to draft to revision and then to the final proofreading stage, I pick away at my own work and the projects of others that I edit. But the editorial "picking" can only start once I have words to work with, and I only have them if I sit down to think, plan, and write. I may not have office doors, but I have a desk, a computer, and a dozen ideas. So I write.

Exploration

Live

You've already been considering how to arrange your space and time for writing. Now, if you haven't already, take some time to determine when you will sit down and write each day or several days this week. Once you have a schedule, anticipate distractions and plan ahead for how to deal with them. (Choose your distraction: laundry, telephone, Facebook, children, dinner, etc. Then a plan: auto-fluff, do not disturb, close your web browser, hire a babysitter, order carry-out.) Tell your spouse or a friend your plan and ask him or her to help you mitigate interruptions. The writing life is full of unexpected interruptions, though, so plan on at least a few of those, too.

Some ideas to manage writing time:

- Some people say your subconscious is better prepared to get to work if you write at the same time and in the same place each day. Consider whether this will work for you
- Set a reasonable and specific writing goal for your scheduled time. Instead of "write that article" think "complete a first draft," or rather than "write the introduction" think "write the first paragraph"
- Try the Pomodoro Technique, which suggests doing a work task, like writing, without allowing distractions for 25 minutes straight. Set a timer if you must. Then enjoy a five-minute break. Stretch, walk to the mailbox, or make a cup of tea

- If the timer doesn't work, try a word-count goal. Keep writing until you reach your minimum. Most blog posts are about 500-600 words in length; essays can be different lengths but might run from 1,000-2,000 words; poems and book chapters, well, that's up to you

Respond

At the beginning of each writing session this week, journal for five minutes about your process. Thinking about *perfection* and *perfectionism,* explore your writing inspirations and fears. Spend only five minutes, so you'll still have time for the other writing you have planned.

Write

You'll be writing a lot this week, now that you've committed to a regular schedule. What to probe? In *Rumors of Water*, L.L. Barkat talks about a writer's nemesis, or "things that hinder our best writing," like The Censor, The Market, and The Procrastinator. What is your writing nemesis? What internal conflicts or external circumstances keep you from a rich writing life? Craft a short essay that describes your writing nemesis and how you plan to face it.

Bonus

Barkat also discusses *balance* in the writing life: "Writing starts with living. Living starts with somebody caring so much about something that they need to drag you out of your writing chair and take you where you'll be surprised to find your words." You will be focused on writing this week, saying "no" to other things so you can sit down and do the work each day. At least one time this week, say "yes" when someone offers to whisk you away from your laptop. Say "yes" and go enjoy yourself.

Discuss
For self-reflection or group discussion.

1. Many people have tried to capture, through metaphor, the essence of sitting down to write. We already mentioned Anne Lamott's *one-inch frame*. You could think of it as *giving birth*, *painting a masterpiece,* or *exploring uncharted waters*. Which metaphors are helpful as you write? Which are not helpful? Can you develop some metaphors to make sense of writing?

2. What are the benefits of being idealistic about the writing life? What about being realistic?

3. Are you writing regularly yet? If not, is it time to set some "requirements" aside and simply begin? What dreams inspire you to write? How can you use them to motivate you to do the work?

4. In *The New York Times* article "Don't Ask What I'm Writing," Mark Slouka says, "If writers agree on anything—which is un-likely—it's that nothing can damage a novel in embryo as quickly and effectively as trying to describe it before it's ready." He goes on to explain the difficulty writers have believing in a work-in-process. They want feedback, but they also cave to the Inner Critic who tries to convince them to give it up. We can relate. Do you struggle with perfectionism? If so, what keeps you from believing your writing is good enough? How might you handle perfectionism? What practical steps can you take?

5. Do you talk to others about what you're writing, when a project is in its "embryo" stage? Have you ever discussed an essay or book chapter too early, too late? Describe a time when you shared about a writing project too early or too late; what happened to the work?

6

Send

I want to publish what I write.

I love my rejection slips. They show me I try.

—Sylvia Plath

Stories

Before I (Charity) started writing professionally, I spent a lot of time wondering where I would submit my work. Having learned about *The Writer's Market* in a college feature-writing class, I scrimped so I could buy the book every year. Sometimes, I would add it to my Christmas wish list, hoping a family member would support a starving artist, since, other than the small salary I earned as a journalist, my writing had not yielded enough income for the casual purchase of a book.

I pored over various markets for hours, listing subjects I knew about and matching them with publishers' guidelines. Nonfiction submissions, I learned, should generally not be written before they were accepted "on spec," so I spent most of my time on query letters. And rather than reading or subscribing to the magazines I queried, I read books about how to submit to and write for magazines.

My work would never get in print if I didn't send it out. So, as a beginning writer, I was all about *the publishing*. Anne Lamott sees this phenomenon with many writers who attend her workshops. "The problem that comes up over and over again is that these people want to be published," she says. "They kind of want to write, but they really want to be published. You'll never get to where you want to be that way, I tell them."

None of the query letters garnered much interest. An editor might ask to see an article, but then later reject it. So while I was waiting for my big break, I started doing other writing. Volunteer organizations and employers learned of my skill and began asking me to submit to their newsletters or help write their brochures. I was happy to do the work, but still, I pinned my hopes on magazine publication.

After years of being rejected by magazines I had never read, I came up with an article idea for a magazine I regularly subscribed to and had enjoyed for years. I drafted and sent the query letter, and as had happened occasionally, the article was accepted "on spec." This time, however, I was writing for an audience I knew: me. As a regular reader, I had a sense of the tone and content of the magazine. To my delight, the editors felt the same way. Within a few months, I was a published writer with a check in the mail.

It is natural to want others to read our work. An entire school of literary theory from the 1960s and 1970s, called "reader-response criticism" claims "the reader is an active agent who imparts 'real existence' to the work and completes its meaning through interpretation." In that sense, our writing is only complete when someone else—anyone else—brings his experience, history, and hope to what we have written.

I see a dubious contemporary trend in my desire for an audience, however, that comes with the instant gratification of blogs, social media, and online commenting. Addicted to rapid feedback, "Publish" has become a button I push so other people will respond immediately to my words. When they like my writing, I feel affirmed.

So affirmed, in fact, that in order to get more feedback, I've posted sub-par writing. Sometimes I forget how much it takes to shape the work. I begin to question the need for editors and proofreaders. I'm frustrated when a piece I slapped together in 30 minutes isn't igniting the world.

When novice writers come to editor and publisher L.L. Barkat, frustrated with their lack of success in getting a book published, she asks, "Would you publish you?" It's a fair question for any publication pursuit. Considering the economic factors involved— the expense of publication and promotion, countered with the realistic expectation of sales—would I take the risk on myself if my investment was financial and not just creative?

I might say "yes!" at least half the time, about my willingness to publish myself. If that's the case, then I should definitely send the work out. But if I've spent more time trying to get published than producing a great article, essay, or book, then maybe the best I could do for myself and potential publishers is to work a little more.

Self-editing can feel tedious. How many times can I go back through the same paragraphs and sentences? But this work of self-editing is as much a part of the writing process as the early brainstorming and initial drafting. My work will be edited professionally after it's accepted and before it's published, but I may not get that far if I don't take the time to wade back through, tightening up wordy prose, removing overused vocabulary, and reading the work aloud for rhythm and flow.

Often, I ride deadlines too closely to self-edit effectively. Even when I have plenty of time, I get impatient to hit "send" or "publish" on a piece I've already hashed out. I do better when I make time for each phase of the process. The world will wait.

~

When I (Ann) left my first job, newly married, my husband encouraged me to figure out what I wanted to do. I filled out interest inventories and filled up journals. Eventually, I realized I wanted to be a writer.

A local freelancer told me corporate work was the way to go, to make money as a writer. I told her I wasn't sure I could write in a corporate style. "Of course you can!" she said. "You just need . . . what's the word? Oh, I know, it's *moxie*! You just go into meetings with *moxie*. They won't know you've never written this way, if you seem confident. You can do it."

Nudging my nerves aside, I made business cards and set out in search of clients, exuding as much moxie as I could muster. Despite my insecurities, I landed a couple of small business clients. I wasn't making much money, but I felt like a writer.

As I continued to build my portfolio, I felt the urge to undertake projects more creative than company brochures. Trying something new, knowing the inherent rejections, felt risky. But if I didn't try, I'd never know whether this kind of writing was my "creative vein of gold," as Julia Cameron coins. Others struggle to understand the degree to which we writers take psychological, relational, emotional, and professional risks in the types of writing we undertake and the places we choose to submit. If we aren't taking risks, we're falling back on the kind of writing that's safe emotionally and commercially, and while I had at that point in my career (and have since) happily written articles that fit a commercial need, I wanted to be the kind of writer Betsy Lerner described when she wrote: "All writers are like bomb-throwers, whether they attack with dense academic prose or jazzy riffs of stream-of-consciousness writing. Every writer wants his words to inflame the hearts and minds of his readers. Every writer attempts to reach across the great abyss, also known as the space between people, with his words."

Using a notecard tracking system, I sent numerous queries to magazines. The post office employees got to know me well. I was the girl who came in with two envelopes to weigh, so I could slip a self-addressed stamped envelope inside the main envelope in order to receive my article or poem back, should it be rejected. The process of sending, waiting, finding my manila envelope in the mailbox, and resubmitting elsewhere took months. I'd only float a few things at a time, like a castaway shoving her heart into a bottle and tossing it in the ocean only to wait. And wait. And wait. I would write far less during those long waiting periods, losing energy, losing hope.

Once in a while, an editor said "yes." On those occasions, I'd dance, propose a toast at dinner, then plop back into my swivel chair with renewed vitality and write something new. The elation would not last long, however, and successive rejections would set me back. The ups and downs of submission were hard to manage, cheered by success and dragged down by rejection.

Mingling the emotional struggle of the writing life with the emotional days of early motherhood resulted in some low-output years. Someone in a high chair would smear puréed spinach on my shirt. I'd sit on the kitchen chair, drop my head in my hands and cry, wondering why I even tried to send my work in the midst of motherhood. The spinach splotch on my shoulder slowly dried. The thought of finding creative success seemed unlikely.

Then, I heard about a one-day writing seminar taught by Holly Miller, who used to work for *The Saturday Evening Post*. I left the kids with my spouse, wiped the dust off my portfolio, pulled on slacks and a relatively clean blouse, and drove to the session craving a boost.

After the official presentation, the room cleared out except for a few stragglers. She turned her attention to me and my big black portfolio. "Let me see," she patted the desk.

I unzipped it and stammered, "Here's some of my work. My kids are all young, and I want to write and develop myself more." She was leafing through the few pages. The stack seemed scrawny. "But . . . you, Holly, you've arrived. You've pulled it off—I dream of one day being where you are now. And you said you did it with kids. I just wonder how? How did you do it?"

She looked into my pleading, buggy eyes and said, "You're doing it. I mean, you've got some nice work here. You're getting your name out there. You're working at it. I think you should feel good about what's shaping up."

Then I observed a shift. She asked how old my kids were. I told her, and her eyes grew distant, almost melancholy. I don't know if that's what it was, but that's what I sensed. "I'm where I am today because I worked long hours full-time when my kids were young," she said. "And now they're grown. You'll still have time to develop your career later, but you only have now with your kids. Your kids are so little, and they're little for such a short time. Right now, I suggest you focus on your children. You'll never regret spending time with them. Keep your finger in the publishing world," she continued. "Just keep your name out there. Submit to magazines, like you are. Keep it going on a small scale, and your time will come."

That wistful look carried me for years. I let her reflective advice reassure me—especially when others were building more impressive careers than mine—that my time would come. I abandoned corporate writing but kept showing up at the post office with my two manila envelopes. The post office employees often asked what I was doing. I'd summon my confidence, stand up straight, and answer, "I'm a writer sending off a manuscript." Then I'd herd my kids back to the minivan.

Somewhere in the midst of parenting and submitting articles, someone suggested I write a book about the intersection (or collision) of spiritual life and parenting. An interesting idea, but I could barely get a magazine to pay attention to me. Why would a book publisher have any interest?

A friend introduced me to her publisher, where I submitted my proposal. Before long, a whirlwind descended. We interacted by phone and email, and then in person, where they expressed concern that I was unknown. In today's parlance, they would say I had no platform. I felt small. They were about to reject my proposal.

A week passed, maybe more. I figured it was over. Then, an editor phoned. She said I could write the book. She sent me a contract—*a book contract*!

I wrote that book and hoped to "inflame the hearts and minds of [my] readers" by "reach[ing] across the great abyss."

When the writing was complete, I went to the post office and shipped the manuscript in a box.

Years later, another book found a publishing home, and I eventually landed two online editing positions. Now, I'm on the receiving end of submissions, editing other writers' words after years of sending out my own. I keep in mind what it feels like to proffer the proverbial manilla envelope.

My kids are older now. I kept my finger in the publishing world and, as a result, enjoyed opportunities that gave me a deeper understanding of the industry as it continued to flex. My projects and positions have prepared me to step into a new role as a writing coach, helping others find the fortitude needed to prepare their queries, articles, proposals, and manuscripts for submission to agents and publishers.

It's been a long time since I stood at the post office, envelopes in hand. But I still coach myself and others to cross the great abyss. No stamps required. Just a little moxie.

Exploration

Live

Research opportunities to submit your work. Depending on your available time and interest, find at least one possible new market.

If you're writing articles, essays, short stories, or poems, start by making a list of the publications you enjoy reading—newsletters, newspapers, magazines, websites, etc.—that publish the type of work you want to write. Find out if any of them take submissions. Look in the masthead of printed materials, scan online materials for "contact us" links, or use a page's search function by typing the word "submissions." Copy relevant email or snail mail addresses and contact names into your journal.

Another way to find markets is to see where writers in your online or in-person circles are submitting. It's easy to go to a writer's website to find that information. Most writers list their writing credits in the margin or on a special page. Ask your friends when you are out for lunch or chatting on the phone. Add these publications to your list, then begin reading past issues and online content in order to understand the tone, voice, and topics the editors are seeking.

A couple of things to keep in mind as you research:

- What topics do you write about? Your subject areas or genres will drive your market selection
- Depending on your writing history, you may want to consider unpaid opportunities that allow you to build your portfolio or explore creative approaches. Alternately, you may want only opportunities that pay at a specified rate if you're trying to establish a freelance career that will support you financially. Knowing your needs and desires may steer you toward or away from certain markets

If you're working on a longer manuscript or a collection of essays or poems you'd like to publish as a book, your strategy may be different. First, you'll want to consider your publication options: everything from traditional publishers (usually accessed via an agent) to self-publishing, as well as the indie publishers and small presses that fall somewhere in between. Research each option to discover submission guidelines that may require an agent, a book proposal, a financial investment, or something else.

You may also want to consider investing in a subscription to the now-online *Writers Market*.

Respond

After researching, journal for at least ten minutes about how you feel regarding the possibility of submitting your work. The list you've compiled may leave you feeling nervous, even if you're regularly submitting your work already. Or maybe you found one really great opportunity you're excited about. Write out your ambitions and fears, including the possibility that you aren't ready to submit anything at all right now.

Write

Choose one of the markets you identified, and according to their genre and subject needs, and based on your interests and research, write an article, essay, short story, or poem to submit.

Bonus

Once your article, essay, short story, or poem is ready to send, draft a query or submission letter or email, according to the guidelines you researched. If you're part of a writing group or know other writers who are willing, have them review your piece to identify any problem areas you may have overlooked. If you don't have others who can help, put your work away for a day or two, then come back to it with fresh eyes for self-editing. When the pieces are ready, seal, stamp, and mail the envelope, or hit send on the email.

If you've been considering writing a book, or have already started writing one, take the next step today in beginning a book proposal according to the publisher or agent guidelines you found in your research.

To get you started, we've included a few resources in Appendix 4 about writing book proposals.

Discuss
For self-reflection or group discussion.

1. Anne Lamott says about writing and publishing: "But I still encourage anyone who feels at all compelled to write to do so. I just try to warn people who hope to be published that publication is not all that it is cracked up to be. But writing is. Writing has so much to give, so much to teach, so many surprises. That thing you had to force yourself to do—the actual act of writing—turns out to be the best part." Do you find you spend more time looking for opportunities to submit than you do writing, or vice versa? Are you satisfied with the balance?

2. In an interview on *The Diane Rehm Show*, actress Shirley Jones recounted her rise to stardom as a Broadway breakout. She was on the cusp of attending college to become a veterinarian when a friend—a pianist—talked her into going to open auditions for the Rodgers and Hammerstein musical *Oklahoma*. She sang three songs with her friend accompanying her on the piano, and the casting director asked her to wait a few minutes. He wanted Richard Rodgers to hear her sing. After Rodgers listened, they canceled the rest of the auditions and took this small-town kid across the street to sing three songs with the full symphony orchestra. Three weeks later, she was performing in her first Broadway show. "I was so young," she said, "I'd been in it such a short time, I thought it happened to everybody. 'Show busi-

ness is easy! I don't know what people are talking about!'" It's the rare writer who catches a rocket to stardom. How does the appeal of overnight success influence your submission process? Does it affect how often or to whom you submit? If you don't achieve overnight success, will this influence your submission process?

3. What timing seems right for the phase you're in: does this feel like the right time to be published? Are you frustrated by having to wait, or does it seem too early?

4. What are the biggest obstacles to sending out your work? Are they primarily logistical? Emotional? Consider ways to overcome the roadblocks.

5. What advice would you give a writer friend who's struggling to submit his work? What questions might you ask, or what tips might you offer?

7

Promote

I want other people to know I am a writer.

Without promotion,
something terrible happens...nothing!

—P. T. Barnum

Stories

In the late 1990s, the editorial team of a publishing house considering my book proposal took me (Ann) to lunch in Chicago. This was my first book, my first time alone in a big city, and my first time eating sushi. Nerves jangled just below the surface—I had to parse California rolls while answering questions about my book. As I was gauging how much soy sauce to mix with the mustard, the person who would represent me to their marketing team asked if I would consider traveling and speaking.

Soy sauce dripping through my fingers, I set down the California roll, wiped my fingers on a napkin, and sipped some water, debating how honest I should be. Then I swallowed and admitted, "I've never spoken anywhere." Secretly, I wondered how I could be away from my young children for long stretches, but I didn't mention that.

"I'm just asking if you'd consider it."

I wanted to write, not speak. The editor sensed that, so he continued, "To be honest, speakers sell books. And we need to know you would do your part to sell as many books as possible. We need to hear up front if you'd consider speaking."

I could see only one right answer. "You know," I began, "I've never spoken professionally in my life, but I could get some training." I was deeply involved in a large church and could get advice from pastors who spoke in front of thousands. "I know people who could help me develop that skill."

"We only ask this because we have one author who refuses to travel at all. She writes well, and we like her books, but we need people who will help us promote. Plus"—and here he paused, waiting until I turned from my California roll to look him straight in the eye—"something compelled you to write this message and share it with a broader audience. Right?"

I nodded.

"I would simply ask," he said, "couldn't you see speaking as another avenue to share that same message? Your words—your message—spoken?"

Although I had been panicking at the thought of speaking when all I wanted to do was write, I agreed. *That makes sense,* I thought. I felt strongly about my book and I could see speaking as another way to spread its ideas.

"I'll do it," I said. "I'll do all that I can."

A few weeks later they gave me a contract, and I wrote the book. After the book came out, I gathered tips from friends who spoke in various venues and implemented their ideas for preparing myself and organizing my notes. I developed a speaking checklist to use when making arrangements with the organizer and venue. I practiced a lot. My first few speaking engagements went well. People talked with me afterwards. They bought books. They thanked me.

In retrospect, that interaction over sushi convinced me that promotion and marketing—whether speaking, radio interviews, social media interaction—are best positioned as an extension of the original book (or story or poem) a writer felt compelled to write down and submit for broader distribution. I must want to reach more people or else I wouldn't want it published— why wouldn't I speak the message, as well, and find other ways to let the intended audience know these ideas exist in print form?

I spoke mostly in small venues, but one time I spoke to a few thousand. I did television appearances and radio interviews. Each time, I kept that idea in mind: the message matters and I want to get it to the people who need to hear it. I looked for other ways I could promote my book, such as sending out press releases locally, regionally, and nationally. These garnered several articles, including one in the local paper, one in our metropolitan newspaper, and several mentions online.

Having grown more knowledgeable and comfortable pointing people to my work, I looked for ways to do the same for others. Promoting other writers became as important to me as promoting my own work, as a way to spread the news of great artists. This created healthy rapport and relationships in an extended community. We could help one another, which expanded each of our messages . . . but mostly it felt fun, like a celebration.

These days, writers still speak and use mainstream media to get the word out about their product and message, but they also tap the power of social media to build relationships and interact with potential readers. They use it to announce new projects.

I love the creativity associated with book releases, Twitter parties that energize followers, and community writing projects that stimulate storytelling around a theme. When a colleague steps out, marks a milestone in the writing life—that's laudable.

I've been watching, applauding, and participating in a lot of these efforts, and regardless of the outcome—whether a promotional effort gains momentum or hobbles along—I've grown concerned with how the process affects those involved behind the scenes. I've witnessed invigorating efforts where a team of people that believes in a book will pour themselves out to tell others about it. But I've also watched friends being asked by authors to communicate about a book release in a way that counters their own platform, like sharing content that's out of sync in style, theme, or frequency with how they routinely communicate.

Would I want my book to hit bestseller ranking regardless of how the efforts affected others?

Bestseller sounds pretty cool, but *best friend* sounds better. I want my friends to trust me, so I try to stay sensitive to what they feel they can do to support my work. I hope they'll always be honest with me. They often delight in participating in promotional efforts, but if I sense I'm asking beyond their comfort level, I'll withdraw the request and try something different. It's a delicate balance between inviting others to share in our achievements—leaning on their generosity and support—and creating a situation where they feel obligated.

Will I tell people about my next blog post or book? Will I share the news and invite a few others to share it? Yes. After all, something compelled me to compose my message. I just don't want to turn friends into my personal promoters. They didn't sign on for that.

~

When I (Charity) first began writing, the only promotion I did was to take a copy of my printed words and show it to my mom. She was my publicist and biggest fan, and her efforts usually brought my work center stage (stuck to the fridge) to a small but dedicated audience (immediate family).

For years, my goal was to write for publications that were successful enough to promote themselves. I didn't have a name. I had to rely on theirs. I was a writer, not a marketing specialist.

That changed in 2006 when I seriously attempted to publish a book I'd been working on for years. I was planning to attend a writing conference, and though I hadn't been to many such events, I'd heard they were a great way to meet editors and publishers. The general advice I'd received for the occasion: have a book proposal in hand at all times.

Not knowing the first thing about book proposals, I did what all writers do when they want to know something: I bought a book, *Write the Perfect Book Proposal: 10 That Sold and Why* by Jeff Herman and Deborah Levine Herman.

One of the "must-haves" of any book proposal, they suggested, was a promotion section. "The promotion section is where you state ways to promote the book upon publication," they said. "In practice, publishers tend to do very little to promote the majority of titles they publish. You are free to offer a rational wish list (including getting on Oprah), but this is not going to catch a publisher's eye, unless, of course, you are already a regular guest or are a celebrity in your own right."

Then, without even hinting at the word "platform" or acknowledging the Internet existed (the book was published in

2001, after all), they suggested three possible audiences a writer might already have and should mention in the proposal: "If you're a public speaker, if the media frequently interview you for your expertise, or if you're well connected and can get prominent people and celebrities to endorse and help promote your book."

I had done enough research to recognize I needed a website and blog and frantically set about creating my own. I mentioned those in the proposal. But, beyond hocking a book, what did it mean to build a platform and promote myself as a writer?

The idea of promoting my writing has always betrayed an ambivalence. The way I see it, there are two sides to most writers—the proud, confident one that says, "My life, words, and thoughts are good enough to write down and share with others," and the insecure, embarrassed one that says, "Why would anyone want to read what I have to say?" I wrestle with these sides of myself nearly every time I write, and it colors my perceptions of promotion.

To build my platform with a blog and a website, I left comments on other blogs or linked to posts by other writers hoping for reciprocation. My efforts felt desperate and self-serving. Yet, sitting in my apartment churning out volumes of work without sharing it felt self-defeating.

I discovered the answer to my self-promotion problem in what L.L. Barkat calls the "Fifteen Years of Writing for Your Grandmother Rule."

> It is not uncommon for writers to seek a large audience too early in their writing journeys. The idea of being published is a dream pro-

> moted by a cluttered market of writing books,
> writing conferences, and vanity publishers . . . .
> I love working with new writers but am often
> surprised at the desire they have to pursue a
> publishing dream when they haven't yet put on
> a small-time cooking show, so to speak.

The "small-time cooking show" Barkat references is the fabricated stage her young daughter created in the foyer of their home, for a pretend cooking show, where she acted out her aspirations long before she'd ever attempt to be an actual chef. Barkat likens this to the years before she was a published writer, when she was drafting letters to her grandmother every week and writing book reviews for a local newsletter, learning her craft in front of the same kind of small audience her daughter had.

"I've heard it said that most successful writers put in about fifteen years of small-audience writing before they begin to work with larger audiences," Barkat writes. Thus her "Fifteen Years of Writing for Your Grandmother Rule."

Seeking incrementally larger audiences rather than looking for overnight fame was something I had to come to terms with. I wrote newsletter articles and blog posts for my church, participated in blog tours with other bloggers, submitted ideas to magazines and websites I liked to read and visit, and in the amazing way I've heard recounted by so many other writers, the more writing I did, the more opportunities came my way.

After 20 years of practice, I'm out of my "writing for grandmother" phase. Part of that transition can be attributed to promotion via social media. Over the past several years, social media evolved into so much more than the blog posts and link ups of my early online days. Marketing professionals in general, and writers in particular, have taken messages of brand and product directly to people through Facebook, Twitter, Pinterest, and dozens more sites gaining market share. The potential audience in those venues makes the temptation to broadcast our messages almost unbearable. Even grandmothers are on social media.

Lately, many of those same marketing professionals and authors have discovered that treating *social* media like *broadcast* media is akin to peddling on a city sidewalk during rush hour. We may get a little attention from a few passersby, but we also risk annoying people. That approach to promoting my work has started to annoy me, too.

The very essence of any author platform is alerting readers to our writing. I offer email subscriptions to my blog; post links on Facebook; include links to articles on my author website; ask friends to share the news of book releases. The readers? They can see through a scam and understand when we are trying to use them. Most, though, are willing to invest in an excellent book or piece of writing that meets a particular need.

As I experiment with old and new methods of promotion, am I reaching only for exposure? Or for a lasting reputation, too? It's up to me to know the difference.

Exploration

Live

This week, identify an online writing community and several bloggers whose nature and work resonates with your personal direction or dreams you want to begin shaping. Read to find common ground and a personal connection. Leave a compliment or ask a question that shows you fully engaged with their story, article, poem or art.

See what happens. Think of it as a kind of networking, building relationships that may one day be part of promoting your work. Better yet, think of it as finding friends.

Respond

In your journal, write about the barriers you feel to promoting your work or asking others to help promote it. Then explore what makes you uncomfortable about promotional efforts you've seen from others. Finally, describe methods that intrigue and inspire.

Write

Describe a time when you promoted your own work and felt uncomfortable about it later. Consider what you'd do differently next time.

Or, using material from your journal entry as a starting point (see *Respond*), generate practical steps you can take to overcome promotion barriers.

Bonus

Write a simple plan for promoting your work—existing projects such as a blog or e-book, or a future project. Include tangible ideas for how you might connect with others and involve them in the process.

Discuss

For self-reflection or group discussion.

1. "Just as we are suspicious of the gold digger's love for her ninety-year-old husband," says Betsy Lerner, "we view the writer who courts fame with suspicion, as if being serious about your work and being determined to see it disseminated were at cross-purposes. After all, how could a ruthless self-promoter or blatant fame-seeker possibly produce a work of importance?" Respond.

2. Charity described two sides of a writer: one that says, *My life, words, and thoughts are good enough to write down and share with others,* versus, *Why would anyone want to read what I have to say?* Which way do you lean most often? Why?

3. How do you feel about advice like "writing offers its own reward apart from publishing"?

4. How do you feel about promoting yourself? Have you found a comfortable approach or does it feel like shameless self-promotion?

5. Think of promotional ideas that have worked positively and comfortably for you, then share ideas you wish you had avoided. Make a list you can reference the next time you have a project to promote.

8

Discover

When I write, I find myself.

It is impossible to spend your days writing
and not begin to know your own mind.
The page is your mirror.
What happens inside you is reflected back.

—Dani Shapiro

Stories

By the time I (Ann) was 14, I realized the children's department of the local library couldn't provide the depth I yearned for. Shyly, I made it a habit to browse the adult nonfiction shelves for exercise books, vegetarian cookbooks, drawing tutorials, and a series that taught survival skills, in case I ever acted on my dream of living by myself in the woods, like the kid in *My Side of the Mountain*.

One afternoon I glanced through books on writing. A title caught my eye: *Write to Discover Yourself*, by Ruth Vaughn. I looked both ways and plucked it from the shelf, running my fingers over the green cover with a fuchsia gerbera daisy poking out of a pencil cup. It seemed a little wacky, but...

Write. Discover.

I desperately wanted to understand myself, unearth who I was meant to become. And deep down, I wanted to write.

Cheeks flushed, heart thumping, I tucked the book under my arm to hide the title from anyone who might question my desire to write, or ridicule my search for self. I feared my family's response most of all. In a household of word-people—both parents were journalists and my brother would eventually become an advertising executive—I was the vegetarian runner who asked for art supplies at Christmas. Compared with my family, I had never demonstrated noteworthy writing talent. I lost every game of Scrabble®.

Nevertheless, I retreated to my room, tiptoeing up the staircase, and secretly penned responses to the author's writing exercises. I stuffed the spiral-bound notebook far back in my closet so no one would peek.

Over time, I kept a journal and followed instructions to "portrait" the important people in my life, exploring memories, capturing existence. I sat on the hardwood floor of my bedroom and composed a word-portrait of my father, struggling to express the way his resonant voice, rising from deep within his barrel chest, could build and fill—even shake—the house. Or was it just me, shaking? Page after page, the author encouraged me to continue being specific, to use concrete details and metaphor. I poured out stories from my little world.

Digging into yourself requires a depth of honesty that is painful, the author said, but imperative. She quoted a professor who said a writer "is the person with his skin off." This is how I began to decipher my life. On the pages of a journal, I wrote with my skin off—bare, vulnerable.

My journalist-parents didn't write like that, nor did my quick-witted brother. At least, I was pretty sure they didn't. Of my family, I alone seemed to practice this private outpouring of words and deeply personal reflections. With the help of that stumbled-upon writing book, I peeled back layers to stare at my heart and soul. I began, through practice—through pain—the lifelong process of finding myself.

A few years later, my college creative writing classes gave me permission and an avenue to do more work of self-discovery as I wrote poetry, putting words to a confusing childhood. Writing privately helped me process unfamiliar roles, and writing publicly for class gave me an audience to receive and respond. In young adulthood, married with kids, I maintained this practice of writing both privately and publicly, preserving parts of my identity, keeping them from being swallowed into the chaos of raising young children.

Yet this process doesn't always have to be private or painful—in fact, as I've matured into a happier, healthier adult-hood, writing has played a part in many positive self-discoveries. In recent years, for example, I've discovered a lifelong yearning to travel by motorhome—the seed was planted when my great-uncle showed up at my grandma's house with a shiny Airstream™. For several years I researched, read, and wrote about RV travel, following people online who have lived for months or full time in some kind of motorhome or trailer, all the while dreaming I might end up with one myself.

Two years ago, my husband and I spontaneously bought an old RV, and through traveling and writing about our outings, I find I'm a bit of a vagabond who loves the simplicity and curiosity of a mobile lifestyle. One day, we will take off for a long stretch; in the meantime, I travel for a week or two at a time and write about it.

Self-discovery can be deep and emotionally transforming, as has happened privately in my poetry and journals, or fresh and logistically enlightening, as I've experienced in everyday interactions and assignments...and in my RV.

As a writing coach, I've watched people transform in similar ways. One woman experienced emotional breakthroughs after writing about her past. Another felt empowered to move into the next stage of her writing life, preparing to submit her novel to an agent. In my role as a high school writing instructor, I've witnessed students discover the freedom of self-expression; some have taken hold of poetry, writing free verse and form poetry that revealed their inner thoughts and emotions as they wielded words. Often they had fun tinkering, realizing they had the gift of making people laugh.

I, too, continue to find out more about myself. In journals, I continue to tiptoe into the past and boldly process the present. Writing has led to public speaking, something I've learned to do with confidence and humor. (I'm guessing I've been funny. People laugh in the right places!) Reflecting on skills and successes, I've enjoyed my role of writing coach and found new things to write about. I've grieved the death of a friend, working from despair to soul-sustaining strength. More simply, I've revisited old forms of writing, like poetry, which I have studied and taught; and I'm trying out new forms, like memoir, which might shape the person I'm becoming by looking back on the person I've been.

Writing is more than what I do or teach or coach. I discover who I am.

~

The summer I (Charity) received a crushing book rejection and stopped calling myself a writer happened just before I was diagnosed with cancer. I was 36.

During five months of surgeries, chemotherapy, radiation, hospitalizations, and steroid treatment, pain distracted me, symptoms and medication regimens consumed me, and concentration evaded me. I couldn't get back to the computer.

But my state of mind, more than the condition of my body, was the real roadblock. I was afraid. I didn't think I had a future, and words on screen and paper seemed to be a waste of time.

For months, I thought if I were dying, the last thing I should be spending my time on is forming words into sentences, sentences into paragraphs. I didn't give up writing entirely, though. So many people knew about my situation that the easiest way to communicate with everyone at once was to write about cancer on my blog. Many posts were just newsy—another hospitalization, two more chemo treatments, no more radiation. But something else happened, too.

Even though I was afraid for my very life, and I didn't feel like writing, giving words to the horrors of cancer provided a way for me to face my fears of dying and being dependent on others, to wrestle with the insecurities of losing my hair and losing myself, to fight for hope beyond hospitals.

As my story kept unfolding (since my diagnosis in 2007, I have had three minor recurrences), my writing became more frequent. I continued working out what it meant to be a cancer survivor, but also discovered more about myself, like how fear could tempt me to stop living if I didn't face it in all areas of life.

Eventually, the words began to teach me their importance, to lead me deep into myself. Writing over and over about "empty" and "place" and "hope" also forged the way out. I could fight cancer and continue living and writing and growing. Even in the face of death.

During those months, I learned intimately what Annie Dillard has said, "Write as if you were dying." It's more than apt. Writing is never a waste of time. The struggle and the difficulty prove writing's worth, not its vanity. It's the flirting with writing that felt empty, the sidling up all lipsticked and perfumed but never actually giving it my heart. I needed to be all in.

"At the same time," Dillard goes on, "assume you write for an audience consisting solely of terminal patients. That is, after all, the case. What would you begin writing if you knew you would die soon? What could you say to a dying person that would not enrage by its triviality?"

By being acutely aware of my mortality, and by proxy, that of any possible reader, my writing took on urgency. Life is short. If I'm going to spend my time writing, I want to be skilled. I want to write about important things, or about seemingly insignificant things in important ways. Not that I can't play with words, or create laughter with turns of phrase, or use sarcasm to make a point...if that's where my writing life takes me.

Several months ago, LW Lindquist wrote a guest post for my site about the decision to stop blogging. The choice was made carefully, over time; blog writing was slowly replaced by writing for no audience at all.

"The writing is awful; the exploration, deep and necessary," Lindquist writes. "The words were not written to be read. They were written to be written. They may be among the most important words I've ever put to paper, yet they sit unread in a big white envelope."

Some of this personal writing may be part of a published piece later, says Lindquist. Then again, maybe the words will never have a life outside the seal. It's okay. Publication wasn't the point.

It's a whole new take on putting our work in an envelope.

Exploration

Live

Spend some time in a local cemetery and consider some of the lives that have passed. Imagine what stories they told and were told, stories they carried with them to the end and stories they wish they'd revealed. Think about stories you've told and were told, stories you carry with you and stories you want to tell.

Or, look through old family photographs of loved ones who have had health scares or have passed away, and remember some of the stories they told and the stories you wish you had told them.

Respond

"Write like you're dying." Journal about what that feels like and what it means to you. Write to unfold more about yourself.

Write

Write a short story, short essay, or poem you would send to a dying person, that would not enrage by its triviality...perhaps something that came to you in the cemetery or while turning the pages of the family photo album.

Or, recount (via story, essay, or poem) a time you learned something important about yourself through writing. Alternately, write something you learned about yourself through grief or a brush with death.

Bonus

As a way to balance the tone of this chapter, remember that play can also contribute to discovery of self, enriching the writing life.

Take time to play at least three times this week, considering what it reveals about you. Dance, find a young child to play hide-and-seek, make PLAY-DOH® sculptures with that friend who laughs all the time, or rake leaves and jump in. What feels playful? Figure that out, then go do it. What do you discover about yourself as a writer when you play?

Discuss

For self-reflection or group discussion.

1. What have you learned about yourself through writing, recently or in the past?

2. What areas of your life could you explore further through writing?

3. Does your writing have the sense of urgency or mastery you would expect from someone who is dying? Why or why not?

4. Writing in the privacy of a diary, we can say whatever we want

without affecting anyone but ourselves. Is that an acceptable part of self-discovery? What if that same kind of style spills into an essay for publication? Would that be considered self-indulgent writing, or honest and forthright? What's the line between writing with passion, pouring out the self, and writing in a way that comes across as self-focused? Do we need to avoid self-indulgent writing? If not, why not?

5. How can you sneak past your inner censor to let true and meaningful writing find its way to the page?

6. What have you discovered about yourself through play, delight, and uplifting events or seasons of life? Has writing been part of those experiences? If writing wasn't involved at the time, would you want to plumb those discoveries now?

9

Engage

*I interact with writers, artists,
and others who support my writing.*

It is not often that someone comes along
who is a true friend and a good writer.

—E. B. White

Stories

One evening in the fall of 1995, I (Charity) joined the singles group from my church for an outing at a pumpkin farm. We roasted marshmallows over a bonfire, told ghost stories on a hayride through the woods, and drank lots and lots of apple cider.

That night I also met Maurice.

Although I was an aspiring writer and considered myself to be quite the Creative, I didn't know any other writers, actors, or painters. My friends were medical transcriptionists, nurses, and pharmacists. So when Maurice said he was a writer, I knew we would be friends.

"We should hang out sometime and write together," I said. In hindsight, that probably seemed more like a pickup line than an invitation to talk shop.

As it turned out, Maurice writes horror stories, and I write creative nonfiction. Both of us were early in our writing careers, and neither knew many other writers. We became fast friends.

We attended a writing conference together in Louisville; swapped stories; shared writing ideas; took excursions to bus stops, shopping malls, or emergency department waiting rooms. We were there to blend in and take notes. Secretly, we were hoping a muse would show up, or maybe a publisher with a writing contract.

Despite our differences in genre and writing style, having a writer friend was critical for me in those days when I grew despondent with every rejection. Maurice experienced earlier success than I did. He's more naturally gifted in networking and navigating the publishing industry. Unfortunately, moves, marriages, and job changes have kept us from meeting in quite some time, but having Maurice as a friend set me up for a lifetime of seeking out other writers.

A couple years after meeting Maurice, I found myself in a new city with few friends—none were writers. I happened to see a notice in the public library newsletter about a writing group that met each month, so I joined. One of the members also met with writers at the local Barnes & Noble. She invited me. I went.

Though I hadn't written much fiction, I took the opportunity afforded by the writing groups and began spinning yarns about characters who had lived in my head for years. The feedback was mostly cordial and fairly lightweight, but I was writing regularly and improving by seeing my errors through the work of others.

A few years and a couple of publishing credits later, I was living in another new city. A friend introduced me to a woman who coincidentally had been published in one of the same magazines I had. We met on a regular basis to share tips and encourage each other. Soon, I started a blog and attended a writer's conference, which led me to an online community of writers and artists from all over the world. Curiously enough, this translated to meeting writers in my own backyard, like Ann Kroeker and the women in my present, in-person writing group.

Getting to know other writers can feel a lot like getting to know people in general: the relationships provide camaraderie but have the potential to be competitive. That is, if I choose to see them that way. There will always be writers more talented, more successful, or luckier than I am. But am I really competing with them?

Poet Jeanne Murray Walker says we shouldn't think of writing that way, that there aren't just winners and losers. "It's not a zero-sum game," she said at a writing festival I attended. "Readers have many tastes for many forms. When we create an audience, we create an audience for everyone."

At some point, we can make room in the world, and in our lives, for the presence of other writers. Why not? We will sit next to them at conferences, see their names on Facebook, find their comments on our blogs. We'll recognize their work in the publications that rejected ours. We will buy their books.

And find ourselves in their words.

~

Though my (Ann's) Midwestern city boasts an impressive library, it's not a literary community. To find kindred spirits, I'd attend conferences or drive to a university town to hear lectures and readings. Those outings filled something in me, but I needed more.

One time I returned home from a literary event and announced to my husband that I wanted to move.

"I need interaction like that more than once a year!" My voice filled with longing. "A place where I can mingle with these kinds of people—my people—on a regular basis. Please? Can we think about moving? To a university town?"

Seeing me buoyed and hearing my plea for a change, he soon contacted a university IT department to see if he could find a position, so I could enjoy the acquaintance of literary friends. I envisioned gatherings like the Inklings, a group of writers led by C. S. Lewis and J. R. R. Tolkien who gathered to discuss their projects. No IT job opened up, so I considered enrolling in an MFA program as much for the affiliations as for the training. Nothing worked out, however, and I remained in my suburban city, working alone: just my computer, my books, and me— oh, and my husband and house full of kids (whom I surely love).

Still. I hunted for seminars and festivals to attend, and they were beneficial. The Internet started burbling to life with journals that morphed into blogs that expanded into communities. My people began coming to me—not physically showing up at my doorstep, but I'd make one connection that would lead to an-other, and before long I was part of an online community where writers shared strong stories. I wrote and submitted and started to feel energized like I would at writing conferences. More com-munities emerged, and places like *The High Calling* and *Tweetspeak* began to fill the gap.

"I think I found my people," I told my husband. "They're online."

He celebrated this phase of my writing life—relieved, too, I would quit pestering him about moving.

The blogging subculture offered ways to meet writers with similar interests by simply reading and leaving comments at someone's website or creating community projects where limitless people could join and share articles. I would click on links and visit new writers, leaving comments, getting acquainted. I'd gain inspiration and collaboration. It felt like one big party, for writers.

Eventually I began to encounter some of these people in person. Like Charity. She and I became acquainted online, then realized we lived near each other. Soon, we drank coffee at Starbucks for our first across-the-table meeting. Our friendship grew. We started writing together on occasion, then ended up as colleagues on the same editorial team. We co-led an online workshop, and now we've written this book.

The same places online that draw writers often incorporate the talents of other artists. I've met people engaging with and exploring a range of artistic media. Business owner and art-content curator Maureen Doallas. Adventurer Claire Burge. Photographer Kelly Sauer. Their work invited me to risk and dabble, to move beyond the printed page to images and canvas, whether through visiting exhibits or taking up my own brush or camera. I have.

These are a few of the things I imagined would happen when I found my people. And some I never dreamed.

Exploration

Live
Engaging with others in the writing life goes both ways. Identify three people: a person you could support, a person who supports you, and a community you can both contribute to and draw from.

1. _____ supports me.

2. _____ is someone I support.

3. _____ is a community I am/ would like to be involved with. (If you aren't sure about this one, start with *Tweetspeak*! It's a place that really cultivates the lives of writers.)

Then, think of three things you can do to support another artist or writer, this week, like write a letter to an author or take a peer to lunch.

1. _____ person/

_____ action

2. _____ person/

_____ action

3. _____ person/

_____ action

Or, think of three things you could do this week to engage in a community of writers or artists without expecting anything in return. It could be as simple as liking a Facebook page and leaving a positive, specific note or as involved as researching local writers groups. (Your library or local bookstore might be a good place to start . . . writers like to read!)

1. _____ group/

   _____ action

2. _____ group/

   _____ action

3. _____ group/

   _____ action

Respond

Spend ten minutes writing in your journal about a time of lone-liness as an artist. What did you long for? Be specific. Describe how you moved through that time. If you are still feeling artisti-cally or creatively isolated, explore how that affects your writing life, your creative process, or your sense of accomplishment.

Write

Write about a time you interacted with other writers. Tell a story about meeting them at a conference or in a writing group. Describe how you felt when you made that connection. Did the encounter go as you'd hoped? What went well in your interaction with other writers? What didn't go so well? What are you looking for as you continue to make creative connections? Use first per-son, even if you choose to write a poem or short story; include as many details as possible.

Bonus

Explore ways to write collaboratively this week. It could be as simple as inviting a friend to a coffee shop and working on your own projects at the same table. Or maybe you could participate in a *Tweetspeak* prompt, joining others in writing about the same topic all at the same time. If you really want to explore collaboration, consider co-writing an article, blog post, or book. Take the first step by talking with other writers about what collaboration means to them.

Discuss

For self-reflection or group discussion.

1. While the writing life can be rich and rewarding, disappointments and difficulties also arise. Do you have a support network that can help you ride the waves of both success and failure? Which people support you the most? How are they there for you in the highs and the lows?

2. Have you found "your people"? What are they like, and where did you find them? If you haven't yet found them, describe your ideal set of companions. Where do you think people like this can be found?

3. You've identifed where "your people" can be found. What step can you take this week to move yourself into those spaces? If you're already among your people, is there someone you know who could be invited to join you, to get him or her on the path toward artistic and creative companionship?

4. Anne Lamott says some writers sign up for workshops or creative-writing classes to learn to write or write better, receive feedback from real-life readers, share successes or disappointments. "A certain kind of person finds writing classes and workshops to be like camp, and just wants to hang out with all these other people, maybe with a writer he or she respects, to get and give response and encouragement, and to hear how other people tell their stories." What are you looking for in your interaction with other writers?

5. Have you ever written collaboratively? What were the challenges? Any good surprises? If you haven't written collaboratively, what has kept you from it? If you could co-write with anyone at all, who would it be and why?

10

Plan

I am intentional about my next steps.

Arriving at one goal is the starting point to another.

—Fyodor Dostoevsky

Stories

I (Ann) traveled out west the summer of 2013. As my family and I barreled down a New Mexico highway through a barren landscape, we saw a storm. Winds, like a giant, invisible broom, swept sand up and around. *Swoosh!* Currents pushed against the side of our vehicle, and debris shot across the road.

"Look!" I pointed. "A tumbleweed!"

It hopped over the fence and bounced like a beachball twice to cross the highway, before soaring high over the fence on the other side, disappearing into the swirling dust. I had to shout over the roar of the wind for my husband to hear. "I always wanted to see a tumbleweed, but I didn't realize I'd see it under these circumstances!"

I'd only seen tumbleweeds in movies and cartoons. This was my first glimpse of the real thing, and realizing that its movement depended on violent, threatening gusts, I decided to stop comparing myself to a tumbleweed. In my Midwestern mind, tumbleweeds had seemed sort of go-with-the-flow, lazily rolling across the desert in whatever direction a puff of wind might send them. That's also how I viewed my life as a writer. I didn't plan my direction much or set definitive goals; I just went where the wind blew.

But watching that storm hurl the hapless tumbleweed, I realized I didn't want to be blown completely off the path. I wanted enough control to dig in and stay for a while, especially if I liked where I'd landed. So I've abandoned the tumbleweed analogy in favor of something more stable (if overused): my writing life these days is more like the habit of keeping a garden. I sow seeds, watch for growth and fruit, nurture what's flourishing until it seems the harvest is fading, and a sow a new batch of seeds when the time is right.

I edit content for two online communities, submit my work to websites and magazines, collaborate with other writers, coach high school students and adults in their craft, and publish articles at my own website. I intentionally work this literary garden on my own and with others.

My fellow gardeners inspire me to plan and set goals. They model risk-taking and organization, tackling new projects and integrating the latest technology. Thanks to the encouragement of others in this broad community of writers, I'm more organized and deliberate. When looking at a project, I break it into manageable tasks and schedule them to pace myself leading up to the deadline. I use a task management system that serves as a to-do list for each day and coordinates with a calendar. I wake up, accomplish my daily routines, and sit down and do what my system tells me to do. Because that's my plan.

In the early days, I could never quite see the big picture through the blustery dust of the tumbleweed approach. When I stopped being buffeted about, I was able to schedule my weeks and days to align with the vision I have for my writing life. I developed a long-range plan, hoping to look back decades from now and say, "I'm glad I invested in the creation of that work," instead of, "What was I doing all those years?"

My planning isn't perfect; unexpected events, both good and bad, can throw me off. Nevertheless, my writing life is taking root and growing; I'm making significant, measurable progress each day. I still leave room for serendipity—a phone call from an event planner looking for a conference speaker, or a publisher wanting to hire a writing coach to work with one of their writers, or a magazine editor requesting a 2,000-word article on a topic of my choice.

Clarity. Vision. Organization. Planning. I'm not waiting for the writing life to randomly bounce across my path. And if the wind whips up a surprise for me, I'm ready.

~

A couple of years ago, I (Charity) realized I needed to take my writing to the next level. I'd been toying with writing, but it might be time to build something more complex. What did that mean?

It was the end of May, and I received an email from my friend Amber: "I really want to work on my writing this summer.…If you can think of any writing thing to work through together to get better I would love the suggestion."

I was intrigued. Certainly I was not under the delusion that my writing was perfect, that I had nothing further to learn. I had been thinking, myself, about experimenting more with collaborative writing. I clicked through to a blog post Amber referenced in the email.

Author Russ Ramsey discussed the story of master Dutch painter Rembrandt Harmenszoon van Rijn. Though the world knows Rembrandt as one of the greatest painters in history, he was acutely aware of his limitations, that he couldn't "paint the way they want me to paint."

Rather than focus on what he couldn't do, he became a master at what he could: painting to become the best Rembrandt he could be. To what end? Ramsey offers:

> For what? For mastery. And why? For joy, because the mastery of something leads to a greater enjoyment of it. Singers, musicians, painters, writers, athletes and artists of all stripes know this. The harder we work at something, the more we are able to enjoy it. Rembrandt knew it too. Later he would advise, "Practice what you know, and it will help to make clear what now you do not know."

I've been writing long and often enough to realize what I can't do. Yet I had not been inspired to take what I *can* do to the next level, to do the work of being the best writer Charity can be.

Initially, I started reading more about how to create great writing. Then, I started blogging about what it meant to do great writing. Eventually, I stopped reading and thinking about it and tried doing it. I set out to become a master writer.

To do so, I had to have a plan.

Desire was step one, but it needed specific actions to propel me. I decided to limit my blogging in favor of submitting my work to outside publications more regularly. I knew the process of having my work evaluated by editors would help me improve. I also decided to expand and narrow what I was writing about. On my blog, I wrote about anything that struck my fancy, but I wasn't writing about art and culture. Not only could I integrate those topics into the places I was already writing, I could also pursue additional opportunities.

Then there was form. I have long considered myself an essayist, but I began exploring form more seriously, trying to write within the boundaries of what many consider a good essay. At the same time, I realized the wordsmithing of poetry and the narrative arc of fiction could help develop master writer qualities. So I included occasional short stories and poems in my writing, and reading. I wasn't going to change the world with my writing plan, but I hoped to become a better writer.

What would I write about? Nearly every plan for my writing life brings me to this question.

Since I wasn't blogging as much, where else could I write about the minutiae of my life, like the trash I found in the storm sewer in front of my house or the way my puppy spun circles in the swimming pool in the back yard? The little topics that struck my fancy now needed to be set aside or, if I planned well, integrated into a larger work. Would I have enough to write about that was worthy of submission?

Annie Dillard says that when a writer is working on a piece, that's not the time to squirrel away bits of the inspiration for later. We can plan projects and predict pieces we will write, but the inspiration can't be saved.

> One of the few things I know about writing is
> this: spend it all, shoot it, play it, lose it, all, right
> away, every time. Do not hoard what seems
> good for a later place in the book, or for another
> book; give it, give it all, give it now. The impulse
> to save something good for a better place later
> is the signal to spend it now. Something more
> will arise for later, something better.

At the same time, some stories can't be written now. They don't
fit together, or they compete. Says L.L. Barkat, "Sometimes as
writers, we want to gather everything into a single place. We can't
fathom the idea that it is okay for something to go missing in an
article, a poem, or a book. I have wanted to tell all of my stories
in one book, as if a single book could really hold all my stories."

Or maybe the stories refuse to be written. Either the story is
not ready, or I'm not ready to tell it. Do I proceed anyway, as Dillard seems to suggest, or is there room to wait, as Barkat asserts
—not because I am saving the best for last, but because it won't
be good? Not yet.

Barkat assures, "There is no hurry. The things we cannot
write about today, we will surely find we can write about tomorrow.
We should not worry about the process, but simply trust it and
move on."

In other words, having a plan doesn't mean having all the
answers. It simply means painting a door. And another, and another. For a writing life that lasts.

Exploration

Live

Consider the systems you have in place to support your planning process. You may want to start with pencil and paper to jot notes as you think about your long-range plans. Later you can expand to systems that organize, track progress, and help you set goals and deadlines. Talk with people like your spouse or business partner, whose lives will be impacted by your long-range goals, to get input and ideas as well as initial reactions, so you know if you'll need to manage their expectations over time, gain support, or redefine the relationships.

Respond

Respond to this prompt in your journal: "Right now, I see myself primarily as a/an _____ [essayist, poet, blogger, novelist, humorist, micro-blogger, etc.], and/but the writing I would love to do next is . . . "

Write

Think back to something you planned in the past. Describe through narrative how the plan went, how well you stuck to it, and what you've learned about planning.

Bonus

Write a letter to yourself expressing your desires and plans for your writing life for the next months, years, and beyond. Describe accomplishments and activities, workspace and relationships, projects and bylines. Include as much detail as you like, then date it, fold it up, place it in an envelope, write your name on the outside and date it again with today's date and a date six months from now.

Place the letter in a desk drawer or special folder and mark your calendar for six months hence. Plan to open the letter and see where you are in comparison with your plans, then mark your calendar for another six months and so on. You might want to write more letters at each six-month mark to add to the collection, but leave this initial letter in the envelope to revisit.

Discuss

For self-reflection or group discussion.

1. What's been your approach to planning your writing life up to this point? Are you the type who likes to create long-range plans and work on specific goals along the way leading up to weekly, monthly, yearly, five-year, ten-year plans, and lifelong plans? Or do you prefer to follow serendipity? Give an example.

2. What planning approach would most effectively drive you toward your writing goals? Is it the approach you're taking now? If so, how can you improve it?

3. What's the big dream for your writing life that feels like it will never happen, or like it won't happen for a long time? Is anything specific standing in the way? What's the next thing you could do to make progress toward that dream? If you don't have a big dream, what's the next thing you can do today to simply make progress in your writing life?

4. What would a "master writer" look like to you? Are there

aspects of your writing that capture this now? Where are the holes? What steps can you take to strengthen your unique masteries? To fill in your mastery gaps?

5. How do you know if a story is ready to be told? Does it need to be ready for public telling, in order to begin? Where, in fact, do you believe a story starts?

11

Rest

Sometimes, I stop for a while and do other things.

In these thirty years I have made a strict point
to take lavish periods away from writing,
so much time that my writing life sometimes
seems to involve not writing more than writing,
a fact I warmly approve of.

—Richard Ford

Stories

"Bring something that has inspired you in another medium—music, photography, art, 3D art, science, history, nature, etc." This was Amber's challenge to our monthly writing group. The month before, several of us had brought books that inspired our own work. Now, we were supposed to look outside of words.

We went around the circle, each talking about the inspiring flowers or music or curious object we brought. I (Charity) pulled out my new membership card from the local art museum. Jen displayed a paperweight. Kelli surprised us when she said the thing that most inspired her writing in the last week was "not writing." After an intense season of writing deadlines and editing projects, time spent away from words energized her, then drew her back to writing.

Despite my initial surprise, I realized I, too, have experienced this, though my time away from writing usually results from circumstances more than design, when an overscheduled calendar or an extended illness draws me out of my normal routine. Whatever the cause, time spent *not writing* gives me more moments to live and explore. During those seasons, I often stockpile ideas without even realizing it. Though I'm not writing a word, I begin to gradually think in sentences and paragraphs again. Before I know it, I'm rested and eager to get back to the laptop.

Rest reminds us that though we are writers, we are also human. We need breaks. If I want a sustainable writing life, sometimes I need to sneak away from the laptop and go eat a bowl of ice cream. Maybe even every day.

This morning as I write, I have a summer cold. I tried getting extra sleep last night, hoping to halt the inevitable. I've been drinking water and avoiding sugar. My husband and I have a short road trip planned for the afternoon, so I took a decongestant, hoping we could still go. I'm actually feeling a little better.

Should I turn off the laptop, cancel our plans, and lay in bed for a couple of days? I wonder. I am working under deadline on the curriculum for an online workshop, and this weekend trip to visit with my brother and his family has been planned for months. It's the only time we were all free. This time, I will choose to keep working.

Next time, I may need to stop. I can't live a constant life of deadlines and busyness without consequences. My cold, in fact, may be the result of how I've been pushing myself.

If I don't rest, my writing will also start huddling under a blanket, in bed with a summer cold. I have to give it time to recover. Or, on a regular basis, I could just grant myself a break.

Annie Dillard recounts the summer she was writing the second half of *Pilgrim at Tinker Creek*, working long hours, not even stopping to watch the Fourth of July fireworks.

> During this time, I let all the houseplants die. After the book was finished I noticed them; the plants hung completely black dead in their pots in the bay window. For I had not only let them die, I had not moved them. During that time, I told all my out-of-town friends they could not visit for a while.... the fanaticism of my twenties shocks me now. As I feared it would.

I know a lot of writers. I read their blogs and follow their Facebook posts. Those two outlets alone usually reveal who's under deadline or who's taking a break. We apologize for our absences. "Book deadline tomorrow! This deadline has been the main reason why I've pretty much disappeared from reading blogs, writing for my own blog, and answering email for the past few months. I'm both enjoying the process and looking forward to catching my breath." Shortly after this friend's status update, we began to see life again: a post about his vacation location, links to articles (he must be resting: he's reading again!), and then eventually, he's back writing blog posts and commenting on Facebook.

The writing life is rewarding. Anne Lamott calls it a "gift" to find a place in the writing world. "Being a writer is part of a noble tradition, as is being a musician—the last egalitarian and open associations," she writes.

Sometimes the gift looks like *rest*.

~

My (Ann's) writing life is so woven into the rest of my existence, I'm always experimenting to find a sustainable rhythm, knowing it will evolve as I enter new life stages. I need time for play and people, exercise and eating, refreshment and rest. To that end, I spend time with my family and have lunch with friends; I follow interests to satisfy my curiosity; I delve into new technologies.

Sometimes I need a complete change of pace. A hard stop. It's challenging to stake out a break, especially when facing deadlines.

The summer of 2013, I hesitated signing up for family camp. Letting go of this annual tradition would disrupt our family's expectations, but I wasn't sure I could spare the time to retreat into the piney woods of Michigan's Upper Peninsula for a full week of doing nothing. I needed to read, research, write and rewrite, and turn things in before September. Camp would swallow the last week of July and the first days of August. And it offers iffy Internet access.

The kids begged to go—they had no deadline—and my husband and I debated. Maybe I needed the respite—after all, we were still grieving the death of a family friend and managing issues associated with my extended family. Pulling away for a week could give me emotional space, though I wouldn't clock significant work hours (which made me anxious!). Finally, I agreed to go. I packed up backpacks and bags full of books and my laptop, and we drove north. At camp, I sat a lot, often with a book but just as often with nothing. I sat at a picnic table. I sat in an Adirondack chair. I sat on a beach towel on the sand, on a couch in the lodge, and in a folding chair by the calm, cold water of Lake Huron.

Evidently I needed to sit and do nothing almost the entire week. One morning, however, I vacated my chair and jogged through the woods on a trail cushioned by pine needles. Through the trees I caught glimpses of shoreline, and halfway through the run, the path opened up to a sandy cove where I stopped and stretched and stared, breathing in the less-polluted air and feeling the release of so many months of strain. I jogged back and sat some more.

To experience this kind of extended mental rest was unusual. When the week ended and we drove home, I truly felt restored. I returned to my desk and churned out content to meet my deadline more robustly than I might have if I'd stayed home and barreled through.

The deluge of words made possible by social media had not even begun to pour into our lives when Dorothea Brande observed, in *Becoming a Writer*, that we are forever reading and writing, never resting enough to let our minds be generative. She noted that prisoners who've never written a word in their lives start grabbing paper and furiously pouring out their thoughts and feelings, once the bars close them in; people staying in hospitals snatch whatever they can find to read or write. Her unexpected conclusion? "If you want to stimulate yourself into writing, amuse yourself in wordless ways." She suggests rhythmical, monotonous, wordless activities—ones which disengage the mind—to release the solution to a writing problem.

When my writing mires down and I need perspective or inventiveness, I churn out enough words to compose my way past the predictable. That doesn't always work. Sometimes, instead, I jog and let my mind wander as I fall into that steady rhythm of soles against pavement. *Slap*, silence, *slap*. Other times, I crank some music and dance or spin my hula hoop. I might leave my writing space and wash dishes, wipe the counter, or perch on the white metal porch chair and stare at the fir trees out front.

My journalist mother said she often did the same thing and found it impossible to explain that even when she was standing and staring—not rattling the typewriter—she was still working. She had to build in *thinking time*—or *non-thinking time*—when the brain could sort. Apparently I would interrupt, yanking her from her reverie.

The same thing happens to me a generation later, as family members see me sitting back in my swivel chair where I appear to be daydreaming. They ask questions, breaking the restful spell. I don't bother to explain I'm working. And? It might bring my mother a certain satisfaction to know it's come full circle.

I should take her to the pines. If you need a rest, come along.

Exploration

Live

Experiment with the concept of an "artistic coma," a phrase coined by Brande. (Read McInerny's, "Don't Call an Ambulance. It's Only an Artistic Coma," for more details.) Before your next writing session, find a quiet place where you can be alone. Do nothing. Remember, the goal of this particular exercise is to clear your mind so the writing will flow almost effortlessly.

Or, explore mini-breaks or rhythmic, non-writing activities during your writing sessions this week. Take a walk around your neighborhood, chop vegetables, wash the car, shovel snow, or sit on the porch and sip a cup of tea.

Respond

When the urge to write overtakes you in your artistic coma, to the point where you can no longer resist, freewrite in your journal for ten minutes. Capture ideas, phrases, and thoughts about rest or writing problems you have been struggling with. This is freewriting; follow your mind where it leads.

Or, write in your journal about the mini-breaks you took: did they help? Were you resistant? How could you incorporate more rest into your writing life? Are there dangers of too much rest?

Write

Write a short essay, story, or poem about a time when you weren't writing, whether the break was planned or compelled. Why were you not writing? What were you doing instead? How did you return to writing? What did you learn? How did your writing benefit or suffer?

Or, don't write another word for the week. Take the time you would normally spend writing to do something restful. Grant it!

Bonus

Invoking an artistic coma before a writing session is one thing, but planning a significant break is another. Maybe you don't feel you need a pause right now. Perhaps you've been inspired by the writing you've been doing from the explorations in this book and you're hoping to ride the momentum to greater productivity. Or maybe these same activities or other circumstances in your writing life have taxed you in ways you didn't expect, and you need some rest. Either way, consider how to take a planned break from writing. If you have deadlines looming, choose your timing carefully. Will you get away physically/geographically? Will you just avoid the laptop for a few days? What might be the benefits of such a break for you right now?

Jot down in your journal all of your ideas for resting from writing, and plan to implement them after you've completed this book. Or, if you're planning to ride the wave of momentum, save your notes for later, and take a break when you really need it or, better yet, just before you really need it.

Discuss
For self-reflection or group discussion.

1. How hard is it for you to know when you need rest, or when you're tumbling into distraction to avoid the work? What's the difference, or are they possibly related?

2. Are you more of a doer, blasting out a word-count goal every morning and the idea of rest seems counter-productive? Or are you someone who tends toward avoidance, where permission to rest might be permission to skip reaching your goals? What's the benefit of rest for each type of writer?

3. What wordless activities do you already enjoy that you could

turn to when you need a writing break? Which of these, or other activities, can you implement into your process so you're regularly taking small breaks?

4. Are there risks to resting too much? Not at all? What are they?

5. Outline an ideal day (or hour, or week) of resting. Be specific. What pieces of the ideal vision could you implement right now? What parts might require planning? Then implement, or plan.

12

Limit

Because I write, I let some things go.

I wish for you a wrestling match
with your Creative Muse that will last a lifetime.

—Ray Bradbury

Stories

Once, I (Charity) took watercolor lessons from an artist. She was a brilliant craftswoman, with wonderful perceptions of color and light and reflection. Under her tutelage, I learned to let the painting tell me where it wanted to go, to think about negative spaces around objects, and to paint what I see, not what I think I see.

Peggy was a genius, but she also was a joker, eating chocolate, drinking tea, and laughing loudly as she circled the room helping us with our compositions.

"You have some real talent," she told me after the first few nights at her house. I'd been invited to the group by my friend Sarah who'd been taking lessons from Peggy for a while. "If you really want to get better, though," Peggy contended, "you need to start painting every day."

I nodded. *Yes, every day.* I was inspired, and the feedback I was getting from friends on the few paintings I had done fueled my passion. After weeks of sitting down to paint every day, I realized I was no longer writing every day. With a full-time job and a moderate social life, I didn't have time to do both as regularly as needed, to really master both crafts.

Undeniably, the skills I was learning in each—writing and painting—created synergy with the other. The close observation, the emotional turmoil, and the hard work of sitting down to paint or write served dual duty. *Isn't painting so relaxing?* people would ask. *Never*, I thought. As with writing, I toiled over details. I scrubbed the pigment and reworked entire sections of a painting, just like I deleted paragraph after paragraph during successive rewrites. I suddenly realized I would never be able to master two different pursuits. Yet can my writing life really be sustained with writing alone?

In an article in *Scratch* magazine, Nell Boeschenstein recounts a session she heard with Polish author Adam Zagajewksi. He was asked what advice he'd give young writers.

> He got serious and seemed less bored with the question and his own answer than he had seemed just moments earlier. He cleared his throat with purpose. "Don't be just writers," he said, and then repeated it: "Don't be just writers. Be firefighters, policemen, teachers, doctors, chemists, electricians, but don't just be writers." Being writers and only writers, he said, meant you would be stuck in the corral, communing only with the other ponies, when you should be exploring the world beyond the enclosure.

When I took the plunge to become a full-time freelance writer and editor, I pondered this advice from Zagajewksi, how he urged young wordsmiths to not be "just writers." I worried that days spent with words in my home office would keep me from experiencing the fullness of life. (It's a valid concern— I haven't put on make-up for three days.)

On the other hand, my life has its share of activity. I have a husband and sons who rush in each evening with stories from their day, opportunities for the weekend, and news flashes they heard from friends on Facebook. I have clients whose industries require me to research and make inquiries for information I don't already have. I wave at the neighbors as I ride my bicycle to the farmer's market and study the trees along the country roads near our house, trying to find a connection with this new place I call home.

According to Boeschenstein, her own reaction to Zaga-jewksi's advice has varied over the years, but at the end of the article, she concludes, "insularity is the bane of creativity only so far as we allow it to be."

Boeschenstein continues, "The world comes at you with its decisions and coincidences and past loves and future loves and germs and risks and cancers and deaths and births and weather and seasons and cities and roads and fields and forests beyond the property lines of the ranch no matter what."

Because we have only a certain amount of time, resources, and energy, we limit ourselves to make room for mastery. Even after quitting my full-time job, I don't paint every day.

We limit, but we don't cut off.

~

I (Ann) started freelance writing at the same time I was expecting my first child. I chose to stay home with my infants, and as they grew older, I chose to home educate. Those choices placed natural constraints, so I've only known a writing life with limits.

I've tried to appreciate the advantages, manage the distractions and limitations, and integrate my life and my writing so each complements the other. Much of my research in my 20s and early 30s focused on childcare and challenges facing young parents, as I knew next to nothing about bringing up babies. During those years, my blog content, magazine articles, and both of my books emerged from the unfolding of my everyday life and were geared toward parents. Over the years, my available mental space and schedule gradually opened up proportionally to the kids' growing independence. As they required less moment-by-moment attention, I could read for pleasure and study novels, essays, and poetry for high school literary classes I facilitated.

Free time has increased. But? It has equally filled with options that feel endless. Should I commit my time strictly to writing pursuits, or can I learn more French? What about guitar? I'd need lessons, as music never came naturally when I tried to learn on my own. I'd love to improve my photography—maybe I should enroll in a class and pick up new techniques? Voracious curiosity—central to my writing life—entices me to do it all.

My friend Ruth Vaughn told me about her college years, how she happened to be gifted in music (piano and violin) *and* communication (speaking and writing). In the end, she had to choose a major and one, maybe two, minors. Having to decide between equal talents and equal interests—equal loves—she ended up choosing communication. Everything else dropped down a notch. She had to limit herself to fully develop herself.

When Ruth and I spoke about this, I'd already graduated college and was a young adult trying to plan what to do with my "wild and precious life." Ruth said I, too, would have to choose a "major" and "minors" among the interests that wooed me. I chose to major in writing, which meant I would let go of the opportunity to excel in everything else. I couldn't do it all.

I run to stay fit, but not to train for major races. I keep taking photographs, grabbing tips online and experimenting while on vacation, but without signing up for courses or traveling to seminars. If I'm sitting around the table with my kids and someone suggests an origami party, I'll join in, but I won't spend hours trying to figure out how to fold the complicated elk design I saw on the Internet.

I choose to be a writer.

Exploration

Live

Are there limits you need put in place? Are you "majoring" in too many things?

Make a list of your responsibilities, activities, and interests. Include work commitments, family obligations and activities, social or community organizations you participate in, hobbies you enjoy. Everything.

Then, go through your list, grouping like items, and rating each one as Essential, Important, and Optional. (Define those categories in your own way or create similar ones using different words that indicate varying levels of commitment.)

Essential items presumably cannot be altered. You'll have to work with and around these in order to succeed in the writing life.

Important items will be hard to part with, but if you have too many important items in addition to writing, these may be diverting time or attention you could use to master your craft. *Optional* items are ones you could still participate in, but will not commit the time, resources, and energy to mastering, like you will for writing.

Respond

Determine at least one item on your *Important* list you are "majoring" in that might need to be changed to a "minor." In your journal, begin brainstorming what steps will be needed to make that change. Write about why it will be hard or easy to shift, and which people in your life may need to be involved.

Write

In chapter one, we discussed our identities as writers, as well as other identities we've assumed throughout our lives. In this final chapter, we circle back to what it means to be both *writer* and

_____.

Write a short essay about another identity you currently claim (*painter, parent, nurse, teacher*, etc.) and how that identity connects with who you are as a writer. Answer questions like, do I still think of myself as a _____? Will I need to give up being a _____ if I am going to really commit to my writing life? How does being a _____ inform or enhance my life as a writer?

Bonus

Part of limiting ourselves as writers requires active choice. Will I sit down at the laptop and write? Or will I spend time with Facebook browsing or unplanned laundry folding? Beyond the important priorities of life that may keep you from writing, what are the smaller choices you're making, that prevent you from living a fulfilling writing life? Write these down in your journal, and consider the perceived benefits that keep you attached to such habitual choices. Brainstorm practical steps for taking care of the perceived benefits that underly the choices, in ways that will not sideline your writing life and may even create unexpected synergy.

Discuss
For self-reflection or group discussion.

1. Is it important not only to limit *how* you spend your time, but also *what* you fill your mind with, if you want to improve your writing life? What publications, shows, YouTube videos, or social media sites might you need to limit right now? Or, vice versa: which ones should you spend more time with?

2. In chapter three, we discussed the importance of surrounding ourselves with books, people, and activities that inspire writing, yet now we're advising to limit time with publications and media, people and activities. How do the principles in these chapters work together? Even while you're limiting yourself so you can write, what might need to be added to your life?

3. In addition to time, what other limits constrain us? How can we work within these boundaries? How do these constraints hurt our writing life? How do they help us?

4. Are you currently or do you dream about being "just a writer"? How do you think that position could affect your writing life? Do you agree with the advice that writers should never be "just writers"?

5. The things we love or long for often guide us to new and important paths, even in our writing. Is there a difference between a distraction and a beautiful new key? How can we know?

Final Words

We believe you'll experience a richer life because you're writing, and you'll produce richer writing because you're living well. It's hard to have one without the other.

By engaging deeply in your writing life, you're on your way to becoming a master in "fine living"—an honorary degree, of course, but one that will help you become who you really are.

You've read this book, you've done the explorations. Now it's a matter of choosing to keep being a writer. Hard work, yes. A few simple habits. Again and again, your time will come.

And if you happen to cross our paths, which we hope you do, we'll meet you at Starbucks to share a cup of this writing life.

~

You can find us at our laptops or:
annkroeker.com
charitysingletoncraig.com

Appendix 1 - Tools for the Writing Life

To help you manage the details of the writing life, we've compiled a list of some of the tools we use to help us track our submissions, communicate with readers, or stay on task in the midst of multiple projects. We include these because they currently work well, knowing that promising and powerful new apps and programs are released every year that could work better. Use these ideas and the articles we link to as a starting point.

Task management apps. Set up recurring tasks, use reminders and notifications, take advantage of shared lists (if available) for collaborative projects.

- Todoist—a powerful task manager for personal productivity that lets users manage tasks from their inbox, browser, desktop, or mobile device
- Wunderlist—an organizational tool for managing and sharing lists and tasks
- Mac Reminders
- Google Calendar—syncs with many other calendar apps on phones and computers
- OneNote—an electronic notebook for gathering and managing notes (handwritten or typed), drawings, screen shots and audio commentaries

Time management/Productivity methods. Use one or a combination of these methods to keep yourself productive over long stretches of time.

- Pomodoro Technique
- Seinfeld Method
- Mac Calendar
- Google Calendar

Submission trackers. Ann and Charity use self-invented methods of tracking submissions based on Excel Workbooks or Google Sheets. We also offer some apps recommended by others.

- Google Sheets
- Hey Publisher

Idea and detail tracking/capturing. When an idea hits you or an engaging scene arises, it's helpful to have a method of capturing those details. Here are a few ideas.

- Note cards and pen always at the ready
- Smartphone voice memos
- Phone camera, iPad camera, or regular camera. Upload your photos to Evernote workspace, or if you take a picture of a placard, building description, or book title, you can type that up in your notes as well
- Type or dictate your notes, or transcribe voice memos into the content management application of your choice
- Apps for capturing your content—Notes, Evernote workspace, Google Docs or Sheet, Excel Workbook, or OneNote

Collaborative writing tools. If you're working with other writers on a joint project, consider these tools.

- Google Drive—Ann and Charity used Google Drive to compose, edit, and collaborate on this book. Documents can be shared, users can work simultaneously, comments and edits can be added and tracked. We both use Google Drive for individual writing projects, too, and Ann uses it with her writing coach clients
- Microsoft™ Word—use the Track Changes and Comment features in Review mode
- Draft—an application for managing version control and collaboration

Project management. Task management apps and systems may be all you need, but when things get more complicated, you can look into project management systems.

- Toodledo—a collaborative, to-do list that integrates with web browsers, mobile phones, and your calendar
- Asana—a web and mobile application designed to enable teamwork without email
- Basecamp personal—an online project and content management system

Business management. Depending on the type of writing you pursue (such as corporate freelancing) and the degree to which you develop your writing life, you may want to look into some business tools to stay organized, especially if you're running your writing life as a business and filing taxes as such.

- Invoicing tools
  - Excel spreadsheet
  - PayPal invoicing
  - Hiveage
  - Use templates to make invoices via Word to create, print, and send
- Money Management
  - Mint
  - Track writing mileage and expenses in spreadsheet
  - Scan receipts into Evernote workspace or OneNote and/or store in files or boxes

Website and Blog tools. Even if you choose not to blog, writers generally need a basic web presence. Here are some tools to interact efficiently with readers.

- Blogging platforms such as WordPress and Blogspot (also known as Blogger) can get your website started fairly easily and quickly, even if you don't plan to blog
- Web designers who work with writers, such as The Willingham Enterprise, can get your professional site up and running
- RSS feed, Newsletter distribution—MailChimp offers free accounts, provides great templates for emails, and allows you to customize your subscriber list by category. It can automatically send emails when you add a new blog post, or you can schedule special posts that you design and send separately from your RSS feed

Writing disciplines/Practices. Tools to improve writing craft and concepts to develop writing disciplines that keep the ideas flowing and the pen moving.

- Julia Cameron's Morning Pages
- Daily Word Count Goals app—developed to support people who seek an online tool to track their Morning Pages
- Technical writing expertise:
    -Purdue OWL
    -*Grammar Girl* (Mignon Fogarty)
    -Strunk and White's *Elements of Style*

Appendix 2 - Recommended Reading

Rumors of Water: Thoughts on Creativity & Writing by L.L. Barkat, T. S. Poetry Press, 2011.

Becoming a Writer, 1934, by Dorothea Brande, J. P. Tarcher, 1981. (Available free as a pdf)

The Vein of Gold: A Journey to Your Creative Heart by Julia Cameron, Putnam, 1996.

The Writing Life by Annie Dillard, Harper & Row, 1989.

Writing with Power: Techniques for Mastering the Writing Process by Peter Elbow, Oxford University Press, 1981.

On Writing: A Memoir of the Craft by Stephen King, Scribner, 2000.

Bird by Bird: Some Instructions on Writing and Life by Anne Lamott, Anchor Books, 1995.

Walking on Water: Reflections on Faith and Art by Madeleine L'Engle, H. Shaw, 1980.

The Forest for the Trees: An Editor's Advice to Writers by Betsy Lerner, Riverhead, 2000.

Woe Is I: The Grammarphobe's Guide to Better English in Plain English by Patricia T. O'Conner, Riverhead Books, 2009.

The Elements of Style by William Strunk, Jr. & E. B. White, MacMillan, 1979.

The Creative Habit: Learn It and Use It for Life by Twyla Tharp, Simon & Schuster, 2003.

If You Want to Write: A Book about Art, Independence, and Spirit by Brenda Ueland, Sublime Books, 2014.

The Elephants of Style: A Trunkload of Tips on the Big Issues and Gray Areas of Contemporary American English by Bill Walsh, Mc-Graw Hill, first edition, 2004.

One Writer's Beginnings by Eudora Welty, Harvard University Press, 1984.

On Writing Well: The Classic Guide to Writing Nonfiction by William Zinsser, Harper and Row, 1980.

Appendix 3 - Artist Dates

The Artist's Way by Julia Cameron describes the creative impact of Artist Dates.

Tweetspeak Poetry website has a wonderful article describing Artist Dates with instructions on how to embark on your own, as well as samples of Artist Dates, and a book club series that includes a discussion of Cameron's Morning Pages.

Appendix 4 - Resources for Writing a Book Proposal

If you have a great idea for a book or have almost completed one, putting together a great proposal to submit to an agent or publisher is a must. Keep in mind that writing a proposal for fiction differs from non-fiction; the resources below cover one or the other, or both.

"Start Here: How to Write a Book Proposal" by Jane Friedman, co-founder of *Scratch Magazine* and professor at University of Virginia. Access at janefriedman.com.

"Write a Book Proposal That Leaves Publishers Begging to Publish You" by Michael Hyatt, former Chairman and CEO of Thomas Nelson Publishers. Access at michaelhyatt.com.

"The Eight Essential Elements of a Nonfiction Book Proposal" by Brian A. Klems for F&W Media. Access at writersdigest.com.

"How to Write a Book Proposal" by Scribendi. Access at scribendi.com.

Appendix 5 - Resources for Launching a Writers Group

Here are a few resources from around the web that might help you as you take the next step in engaging with other writers. These links primarily direct you to "in real life" writing groups, but online writing groups also can provide value.

"Writing Group Starter Kit" by The Writing Center at The University of North Carolina at Chapel Hill. Access at writingcenter. unc.edu.

"The Good, the Bad, and the Ugly, or How to Choose a Writers' Group" by Holly Lisle. Access at hollylisle.com.

"How to Collaborate—And How Not To" by Holly Lisle. Access at hollylisle.com.

"5 Reasons to Start a Writing Group" by Mark Nichol. Access at dailywritingtips.com.

"How to Start a Writing Group" by Mark Nichol. Access at daily writingtips.com.

"7 Agenda Items for Your Writing Group's First Meeting" by Mark Nichol. Access at dailywritingtips.com.

"5 Tips on How to Run a Writing Group" by Mark Nichol. Access at dailywritingtips.com.

Acknowledgements

Thank you to L.L. (Laura) Barkat, for seeing potential in us and our work, and believing and investing in us for all these years. We'd like to thank Monica Sharman and Lynn House, who read through an early version of this book and offered expert and honest advice. It is stronger and clearer because of your input.

We're so grateful for the encouragement, enthusiasm and support of our two main online communities: *Tweetspeak Poetry* and *The High Calling*. We're grateful not only to our colleagues on the editorial teams but also to every reader who has taken time to read words we've written or edited.

Also, our heart-felt gratitude to the twelve participants who signed up for *The Writing Life* workshop and taught us so much about the role of friendship in the writing life. This book wouldn't exist if we had not sailed off together in the Fall of 2013. Thank you for joining us on that journey, and sharing your lives with us.

Writers may type out words alone at the keyboard, but we can't live this writing life alone. We need people, and we want to especially thank our family and friends, both near and far away, in person and online. You have encouraged us in countless ways over the years, in big ways and small. Thank you for being there, for saying the right thing, for listening as we struggle through an idea or our identity, for faithfully reading our tweets and Facebook updates and blogs, for buying the magazines and books that contain our words. We can't do this without you.

End Notes

Introduction

page 11.   "In her book, *The Forest for the Trees*": Betsy Lerner, *The Forest for the Trees: An Editor's Advice to Writers* (New York: Riverhead Press, 2000), p. 37.

Chapter 1

page 16.   "If you wish to be a writer": Ashton Applewhite, William R. Evans III, and Andrew Frothingham, *And I Quote: The Definitive Collection of Quotes, Sayings, and Jokes for the Contemporary Speechmaker* (New York: St. Martin's Press, 2003), p. 301.

page 17.   "a description of a runner": "RE: Definition of 'runner' and 'jogger'" (LetsRun.com, message posted to thread 4589995 on May 23, 2012, accessed online on July 17, 2014). <http://www.letsrun.com/forum/flat_read.php?thread=4589995>

page 18.   "It was a great moment": Anne Lamott, *Bird by Bird: Some Instructions on Writing and Life* (New York: Doubleday, 1994), p. xiv.

page 22.   "To be a writer": Betsy Lerner, *The Forest for the Trees: An Editor's Advice to Writers* (New York: Riverhead Press, 2000), p. 57.

Chapter 2

page 26. "The secret to all victory": Mark Beitman, "Marcus Aurelius" (*Philosimply* accessed online on July 18, 2014). <http://www.philosimply.com/philosopher/marcus-aurelius>

page 27. "I remember envying author rituals": Barbara Kingsolver, *High Tide in Tucson: Essays from Now or Never* (New York: HarperCollinsPublishers, 1995), p. 96.

page 28. "wears a baseball cap": Barbara Kingsolver, *High Tide in Tucson: Essays from Now or Never* (New York: HarperCollinsPublishers, 1995), p. 96.

page 28. "I felt like Lucille Clifton": Barbara Kingsolver, *High Tide in Tucson: Essays from Now or Never* (New York: HarperCollinsPublishers, 1995), p. 96.

page 28. "From an evolutionary perspective": John Medina, *Brain Rules: 12 Principles for Surviving and Thriving at Work, Home, and School* (Published in 2011, accessed online on July 5, 2014). <http://www.scribd.com/doc/60123148/Brain-Rules-by-John-Medina-Exercise-Chapter>

page 29. "chewing helps concentration": Amy Kraft, "Gum Chewing May Improve Concentration" (*Scientific American*, March 26, 2013, accessed online on Aug. 26, 2013). <http://www.scientificamerican.com/podcast/episode/gum-chewing-may-improve-concentrati-13-03-26/>

page 29. "Tom Hanks claims to be a typerwriter man": Tom Hanks, "I Am TOM. I Like to TYPE. Hear That?" (*The New York Times Sunday Review*, Aug. 3, 2013, accessed online on Aug. 26, 2013). <http://www.nytimes.com/2013/08/04/opinion/sunday/i-am-tom-i-like-to-type-hear-that.html>

page 30. "[T]here isn't any 'right' way": William Zinsser, *On Writing Well: An Informal Guide to Writing Nonfiction* (New York: HarperPerennial, 1990), p. 5.

page 32. "The conflicts of life and work": Wendell Berry, *Standing by Words* (Berkeley: Counterpoint, 2011), p. 22.

page 33. "How we spend our days": Annie Dillard, *The Writing Life* (New York: Harper Perennial, 1990), p. 32.

Chapter 3

page 38. "If you have other things in your life": "Famous Writing Quotes" (*Writer's Digest*, 16 July 2014).

page 39. "I wrote on my blog": Charity Singleton Craig, "Being Specific" (Charity Singleton Craig: Bringing Words to Life, May 15, 2013, accessed online on Sept. 15, 2013). <http://charitysingletoncraig.com/2013/05/15/being-specific/>

page 39. "submitted a review of the exhibit": Charity Singleton Craig, "Ai Weiwei: The Poet's Son." (*Tweetspeak Poetry*, June 19, 2013, accessed online on Sept. 15, 2013).

<http://www.tweetspeakpoetry.com/2013/06/19/ai-weiwei-the-poets-son/>

page 40.   "is careful of what he reads": Annie Dillard, *The Writing Life* (New York: Harper Perennial, 1990), p. 68.

page 40.   "It was to have been set in Tasmania": Geraldine Brooks, "The Writing Life" (Geraldine Brooks [blog], Aug. 14, 2013, accessed online on Sept. 15, 2014). <http://geraldinebrooks.com/news/articles/the-writing-life/>

page 40.   "I will have to learn it": Geraldine Brooks, "The Writing Life" (Geraldine Brooks [blog], Aug. 14, 2013, accessed online on Sept. 15, 2013). <http://geraldinebrooks.com/news/articles/the-writing-life/>

page 41.   "Writers who are intimately familiar": Ben Yagoda, "Should We Write What We Know?" (*The New York Times*, July 22, 2013, accessed online on Sept. 15, 2013). <http://opinionator.blogs.nytimes.com/2013/07/22/should-we-write-what-we-know/>

page 43.   "Reading is the creative center": Stephen King, *On Writing: A Memoir of the Craft* (New York: Pocket Books, 2000), p. 142.

page 43.   "stories of pigs, a chimney fire, and Christmas in Florida": E. B. White, *Essays of E.B. White* (New York: Harper & Row, 1977), pp. 4-5.

page 45.   "Ernest Hemingway modeled his work": Annie Dillard,

The Writing Life (New York: Harper Perennial, 1990), p. 70.

Chapter 4

page 47.   "Try to be one of the people": Dorothea Brande,
            Becoming a Writer (Los Angeles: J.P. Tarcher, Inc., 1981),
            p. 114. (In a footnote, Brande cites James' essay "The
            Art of Fiction.")

page 47.   "the details of the green verandah": Thomas Merton,
            *The Seven Storey Mountain: An Autobiography of Faith, 50th
            Anniversary Edition* (San Diego: A Harvest Book, Har-
            court Brace & Co., 1948, renewed 1976), p. 20.

page 47.   "the man in her neighborhood": Haven Kimmel,
            A Girl Named Zippy: Growing Up Small in Mooreland, Indi-
            ana (New York: Broadway Books, 2002), pp. 121-122.

page 47.   "we learn the name of a teacher": Jeannette Walls,
            The Glass Castle (New York: Scribner, 2005), p. 196.

page 49.   "[S]et yourself a short period each day": Dorothea
            Brande, *Becoming a Writer* (Los Angeles: J.P. Tarcher,
            Inc., 1981), p. 78.

page 51.   "The dump was created in 1996": Indiana Department
            of Environmental Management, "Walnut Creek Land-
            fill Municipal Solid Waste Landfill Permit Application
            Fact Sheet" (Published on December 8, 2011, accessed
            online on July 29, 2014). <http://www.in.gov/idem/
            files/factsheet_walnut_creek.pdf>

page 52.   "Unfortunately for me": Mary Berry, "Wendell and Me: The Home and the Heart Are Never Far Apart" (*Edible Louisville*, June 28, 2013, accessed online on Aug. 24, 2013). <http://ediblecommunities.com/louisville/may-june-2013/wendell-and-me.htm>

page 53.   "Push it. Examine all things": Annie Dillard, *The Writing Life* (New York: Harper Perennial, 1990), p. 78.

Chapter 5

page 57.   "A writer who waits for ideal conditions": E. B. White. Interview by George Plimpton and Frank H. Crowther. "E. B. White, The Art of the Essay No. 1" (*The Paris Review*, Fall 1969. No. 48, accessed online on July 23, 2014). <http://www.theparisreview.org/interviews/4155/the-art-of-the-essay-no-1-e-b-white>

page 57.   "like 'shitty first drafts'": Anne Lamott, *Bird by Bird: Some Instructions on Writing and Life* (New York: Anchor Books, 1995), p. 21.

page 57.   "one-inch frames": Anne Lamott, *Bird by Bird: Some Instructions on Writing and Life* (New York: Anchor Books, 1995), p. 17.

page 57.   "known for her 'morning pages'": Julia Cameron, *The Artist's Way* (New York: Penguin Putnam, Inc., 2002), p. 18.

page 57.   "his 'tool box' of trade tricks": Stephen King, *On Writing: A Memoir of the Craft* (New York: Pocket Books, 2000), p. 109.

page 57.   "talks about a writing schedule": Dorothea Brande, *Becoming a Writer* (Los Angeles: J. P. Tarcher, Inc., 1981), p. 40.

page 58.   "the page, the page, that eternal blankness": Annie Dillard, *The Writing Life* (New York: Harper Perennial, 1990), pp. 58-59.

page 58.   "giving voice to our own astonishment": Annie Dillard, *The Writing Life* (New York: Harper Perennial, 1990), p. 68.

page 59.   "encounter as a girl with the master artists": Madeleine L'Engle, *A Circle of Quiet* (San Francisco: HarperSanFrancisco, 1972), p. 147.

page 60.   "the bottom line is that": Anne Lamott, *Bird by Bird: Some Instructions on Writing and Life* (New York: Anchor Books, 1995), p. 31.

page 61.   "every writer needs a room with a door": Stephen King, *On Writing: A Memoir of the Craft* (New York: Pocket Books, 2000), p. 151.

page 61.   "like an absolutely enchanted writing environment": Stephen King, *On Writing: A Memoir of the Craft* (New York: Pocket Books, 2000), pp. 234-235.

page 65. "Try the Pomodoro Technique": <http://pomodor otechnique.com/>

page 66. "things that hinder our best writing": L.L. Barkat, *Rumors of Water: Thoughts on Creativity & Writing* (New York: T. S. Poetry Press, 2011), p. 42.

page 66. "Writing starts with living": L.L. Barkat, *Rumors of Water: Thoughts on Creativity & Writing* (New York: T. S. Poetry Press, 2011), p. 31.

page 67. "If writers agree on anything": Mark Slouka, "Don't Ask What I'm Writing" *(The New York Times*, Aug. 24, 2013, accessed online on Sept. 2, 2013). <http://opin- ionator.blogs.nytimes.com/2013/08/24/dont-ask- what-im-writing/>

Chapter 6

page 69. "I love my rejection slips": Josh Jones, "Read Rejection Letters Sent to Three Famous Artists: Sylvia Plath, Kurt Vonnegut & Andy Warhol" *(Open Culture*: The Best Free Cultural and Educational Media on the Web, Nov. 21, 2013, accessed online on July 16, 2014). <http://www.openculture.com/2013/11/rejection-let- ters-sent-to-three-famous-artists.html>

page 69. "having learned about *The Writers Market*": <http://www.writersmarket.com/>

page 70. "The problem that comes up": Anne Lamott, *Bird by Bird: Some Instructions on Writing and Life* (New York: Anchor Books, 1995), p. 13.

page 70.   "The reader is an active agent": "Reader-response Criticism" (*Wikipedia*, May 5, 2013, accessed online on Aug. 20, 2013). <http://en.wikipedia.org/wiki/Reader-response_criticism>

page 71.   "Would you publish you?": L.L. Barkat, *Rumors of Water: Thoughts on Creativity & Writing* (New York: T. S. Poetry Press, 2011), p. 118.

page 72.   "creative vein of gold": Julia Cameron, *The Vein of Gold: A Journey to Your Creative Heart* (New York: A Jeremy P. Tarcher/Putnam Book, G. P. Putnam's Sons, 1996), p. 99.

page 73.   "All writers are like bomb throwers": Betsy Lerner, *The Forest for the Trees: An Editor's Advice to Writers* (New York: Riverhead Press, 2000), p. 88.

page 79.   "But I still encourage anyone": Anne Lamott, *Bird by Bird: Some Instructions on Writing and Life* (New York: Anchor Books, 1995), p. xxvi.

page 79.   "She was on the cusp of attending college": "Shirley Jones: 'Shirley Jones: A Memoir'" (*The Diane Rehm Show* broadcast on July 25, 2013). <http://thediane rehmshow.org/shows/2013-07-25/shirley-jones-shirley-jones-memoir>

Chapter 7

page 81.   "Without promotion, something terrible happens": "P. T. Barnum Quotes: Top 19" (The Barnum Museum

Website accessed online on July 21, 2014).
<http://www.barnummuseum.org/pdf/barnum_
quotes.pdf>.

page 85.   "The promotion section is where you state ways":
               Jeff Herman and Deborah Levine Herman, *Write the
               Perfect Book Proposal: 10 That Sold and Why* (2nd ed. New
               York: Wiley, 2001), pp. 25-26.

page 85.   "If you're a public speaker": Jeff Herman and Deborah
               Levine Herman, *Write the Perfect Book Proposal: 10 That
               Sold and Why* (2nd ed. New York: Wiley, 2001), p. 26.

page 86.   "It is not uncommon for writers": L.L. Barkat, *Rumors
               of Water: Thoughts on Creativity & Writing* (New York:
               T. S. Poetry Press, 2011), p. 108.

page 87.   "I've heard it said": L.L. Barkat, *Rumors of Water:
               Thoughts on Creativity & Writing* (New York: T. S. Poetry
               Press, 2011), p. 108.

page 90.   "Just as we are suspicious": Betsy Lerner, *The Forest for
               the Trees: An Editor's Advice to Writers* (New York: River-
               head Press, 2000), p. 79.

Chapter 8

page 91.   "It is impossible to spend your days": Dani Shapiro,
               Still Writing: The Perils and Pleasures of a Creative Life
               (New York: Atlantic Monthly Press, 2013), p. 4.

page 92.   "followed instructions to 'portrait' the important peo-
             ple": Ruth Vaughn, *Write to Discover Yourself* (New York:
             Doubleday, 1980), p. 25.

page 92.   "is the person with his skin off": Ruth Vaughn, *Write to
             Discover Yourself* (New York: Doubleday, 1980), p. 24.

page 96.   "Write as if you were dying": Annie Dillard, *The Writing
             Life* (New York: Harper Perennial, 1990), p. 68.

page 96.   "At the same time": Annie Dillard, *The Writing Life*
             (New York: Harper Perennial, 1990), p. 68.

page 96.   "The writing is awful": LW Lindquist, "In Your Own
             Words: L. Willingham Lindquist - Unread" (Charity
             Singleton Craig: Bringing Words to Life, April 3, 2014,
             accessed online on May 27, 2014). <http://charitysin-
             gletoncraig.com/2014/04/03/in-your-own-words-lyla-
             lindquist-unread/>

page 97.   "Some of this personal writing": LW Lindquist, "In
             Your Own Words: L. Willingham Lindquist - Unread"
             (Charity Singleton Craig: Bringing Words to Life, April
             3, 2014, accessed online on May 27, 2014).
             <http://charitysingletoncraig.com/2014/04/03/in-
             your-own-words-lyla-lindquist-unread/>

page 97.   "would not enrage by its triviality": Annie Dillard,
             The Writing Life (New York: Harper Perennial, 1990),
             p. 68.

Chapter 9

page 100.   "It is not often": E. B. White, *Charlotte's Web* (New York: Harper Trophy, 2012), p. 184.

page 102.   "It's not a zero-sum game": Jeanne Murray Walker, Festival of Faith and Writing breakout session (Calvin College, Grand Rapids, MI, April 20, 2012).

page 107.   "or maybe you could participate": <http://www.tweet speakpoetry.com/category/writing-prompts/>

page 108.   "A certain kind of person": Anne Lamott, *Bird by Bird: Some Instructions on Writing and Life* (New York: Doubleday, 1994), p. 152.

Chapter 10

page 109.   "Arriving at one goal": "Fyodor Dostoevsky" (Christian Classics Ethereal Library at Calvin College accessed online on July 21, 2014). <http://www.ccel.org/ccel/dostoevsky>.

page 111.   "I really want to work": Amber Robinson, personal correspondence, May 31, 2011.

page 112.   "paint the way they want me to paint": Russ Ramsey, "A World Short on Masters" (*The Rabbit Room*, May 4, 2011, accessed online on Nov. 1, 2013). <http://www.rabbitroom.com/2011/05/a-world-short-on-masters/>

page 112. "For what? For mastery": Russ Ramsey, "A World Short on Masters" (*The Rabbit Room*, May 4, 2011, accessed online on Nov. 1, 2013). <http://www.rabbit room.com/2011/05/a-world-short-on-masters/>

page 114. "One of the few things I know": Annie Dillard, *The Writing Life* (New York: Harper Perennial, 1990), p. 78-79.

page 114. "Sometimes as writers": L.L. Barkat, *Rumors of Water: Thoughts on Creativity & Writing* (New York: T. S. Poetry Press, 2011), p. 148.

page 114. "There is no hurry": L.L. Barkat, *Rumors of Water: Thoughts on Creativity & Writing* (New York: T. S. Poetry Press, 2011), p. 153.

Chapter 11

page 118. "In these thirty years": Richard Ford, "Goofing Off While the Muse Recharges" (*The New York Times*, Nov. 8, 1999, accessed online on Nov. 17, 2013). <http://www.nytimes.com/1999/11/08/arts/goofing-off-while-the-muse-recharges.html>

page 120. "During this time": Annie Dillard, *The Writing Life* (New York: Harper Perennial, 1990), p. 37.

page 120. "Book deadline tomorrow": Ed Cyzewski, Facebook post, July 31, 2013.

page 120. "Being a writer is part of a noble tradition": Anne Lamott, *Bird by Bird: Some Instructions on Writing and Life* (New York: Anchor Books, 1995), p. 235.

page 122. "If you want to stimulate yourself into writing": Dorothea Brande, *Becoming a Writer* (Los Angeles: J. P. Tarcher, Inc., 1981), p. 133.

page 122. "artistic coma": Dorothea Brande, *Becoming a Writer* (Los Angeles: J. P. Tarcher, Inc., 1981), p. 160.

page 123. "Don't Call an Ambulance": <http://thecomicmuse.com/uncategorized/dont-call-an-ambulance-its-only-an-artistic-coma/>

Chapter 12

page 127. "I wish for you a wrestling match": "Writing Quotes" (Warren Wilson College accessed online on July 17, 2014). <http://www.warren-wilson.edu/~peal/Writing_Quotes>

page 128. "He got serious and seemed less bored": Nell Boeschenstein, "Not a Complaint" (*Scratch*, October 28, 2013, accessed online on October 28, 2013). <http://scratchmag.net/article/5274a05cc873d951eb2ec91f/not_a_complaint>

page 128. "Insularity is the bane of creativity": Nell Boeschenstein, "Not a Complaint" (*Scratch*, October 28, 2013, accessed online on October 28, 2013). <http://scratch

mag.net/article/5274a05cc873d951eb2ec91f/not_a_co
mplaint>

page 128.   "the world comes at you": Nell Boeschenstein, "Not a
Complaint" (*Scratch*, October 28, 2013, accessed online
on October 28, 2013). <http://scratchmag.net/
article/5274a05cc873d951eb2ec91f/not_a_complaint>

Also from T. S. Poetry Press

Rumors of Water: Thoughts on Creativity & Writing, by L.L. Barkat

A few brave writers pull back the curtain to show us their creative process. Annie Dillard did this. So did Hemingway. Now L.L. Barkat has given us a thoroughly modern analysis of writing. Practical, yes, but also a gentle uncovering of the art of being a writer.

— Gordon Atkinson, Editor at Laity Lodge

How to Read a Poem: Based on the Billy Collins Poem "Introduction to Poetry", by Tania Runyan

No reader, experienced or new to reading poems, will want to miss this winsome and surprising way into the rich, wonderful conversations that poetry makes possible.

—David Wright, Assistant Professor of English at Monmouth College, IL

The Whipping Club, by Deborah Henry (an Oprah selection)

Multilayered themes of prejudice, corruption and redemption with an authentic voice and swift, seamless dialogue. A powerful saga of love and survival.

—*Kirkus Reviews* (starred review)

Masters in Fine Living Series

The Masters in Fine Living Series is designed to help people live a whole life through the power of reading, writing, and just plain living. Look for titles with the tabs **read, write, live, play, learn,** or **grow**—and join a culture of individuals interested in living deeply, richly.

T. S. Poetry Press titles are available online in e-book and print editions. Print editions also available through Ingram.

tspoetry.com

36727953R00100

Made in the USA
Lexington, KY
02 November 2014